Liber Umbrarum

Book of Shadows

LIBER UMBRARUM: BOOK OF SHADOWS
Original copyright © 2013 Pier Luca Pierini
Translation copyright © 2024 Steve Savedow
Artwork © Pier Luca Pierini
All Rights Reserved.

Translated from the original *Il Vero Libro delle Ombre: Liber Umbrarum vel Liber Spirituum Verum Divinum Grimorium* by Pier Luca Pierini, Edizioni Rebis, 2013.

ISBN 978-1-915933-09-6 (Hardcover)
ISBN 978-1-915933-10-2 (Softcover)

A CIP catalogue for this title is available from the British Library.
10 9 8 7 6 5 4 3 2 1

Except in the case of quotations embedded in critical articles or reviews, no part of this book may be reproduced or transmitted in any form or by any means, electronic or mechanical, including photocopying, recording, or by any information storage and retrieval system, without permission in writing from the publisher. No part of this book may be used or reproduced in any manner for the purpose of training artificial intelligence technologies or systems.

Steve Savedow has asserted his moral right to be identified as the author of this work.

Published in 2024
Hadean Press
West Yorkshire
England
www.hadeanpress.com

Liber Umbrarum

vel Liber Spirituum
Verum Divinum Grimorium et Clavis Secretorum

Book of Shadows

or The Book of Spirits
True Divine Grimoire and The Key of Secrets

Steve Savedow
Pier Luca Pierini

With much appreciation to my magical brother, David Rankine, for his support & belief in my work, superior editing, his invaluable expertise, and meticulous dedication to detail.

Contents

From *The Magus* or *Celestial Intelligencer* . . . ix

New Foreword to the English Edition . . . xi

Memorial Biographical Note on 'Caliel' . . . xx

Introductory Note to the Seventh Italian Edition . . . xxi

Historical Introduction to the Fifth Italian Edition . . . xxii

TRUE DIVINE GRIMOIRE (VERUM GRIMORIUM DIVINUM) : BOOK OF SHADOWS (LIBER UMBRARUM)

    Ritual Instructions and Rules of Use . . . 1

    Instructions Relating to the Entire Duration of the Rite . . . 2

    New Moon Rite . . . 3

    Daily Rites . . . 5

    Special instructions for the Three Groups of Lunations . . . 7

    Ceremony of Self-Consecration on the Seventh New Moon . . . 8

    Rules to be Observed after the Consecration and for the Rest of One's Life . . . 9

    The Great Operation for Contact with the Higher Spirits . . . 12

    The Great Operation for the Acquisition of Power over the Princes of the Elements and the Hostile Elementals . . . 17

    How to Deal with the Elemental Spirits and Resist their Subtle Demands . . . 21

    The Nine Rules of Transmitting the Rite to Others . . . 23

    The Familiar Spirits . . . 25

    Appendix: Of the Skills of Evil or Elemental Spirits . . . 26

PREMISE . . . 31

    To the Knights of the Holy Kingdom . . . 33

    The Art of Commanding Spirits of the Holy Kingdom . . . 34

Execution ... 37

Prayer of Request ... 39

The Great Magical Invocation ... 45

Great Magical Operation or Rite of Evocation of the Supreme Spirits ... 46

For Evocation of any other Angel or Genies ... 47

For the Evocation of the Elemental Spirits and the Princes of the Elements ... 47

Psalm 137 ... 50

Consecration of the Sword and Magic Wand ... 52

Invocation of the Book of Spirits ... 55

Invocation to Michael and Figure of the Spirit ... 56

Invocation to Gabriel and Figure of the Spirit ... 58

Invocation to Samael and Figure of the Spirit ... 60

Invocation to Raphael and Figure of the Spirit ... 62

Invocation to Sachiel and Figure of the Spirit ... 64

Invocation to Anael and Figure of the Spirit ... 66

Invocation to Cassiel and Figure of the Spirit ... 68

Formula of Evocation of the Spirits of the Book ... 70

APPENDIX A: Exorcism of Water, Prayers of the Elements, Conjuration of the Four, and Qabalistic Invocation of Solomon (by Eliphas Levi) ... 71

APPENDIX B: Consecration of The Book, from the *Key of Solomon* ... 75

APPENDIX C: Some Pertinent Information from the *Veritable Key of Solomon* ... 77

APPENDIX D: Liber Spirituum, from the *Fourth Book of Occult Philosophy* ... 79

APPENDIX E: Prayers from Preghiera per la Fratellanza Ermetica ... 81

BIBLIOGRAPHY ... 85

From The Magus or Celestial Intelligencer

Book II, Part II (by Francis Barrett)

NOW, if thou art desirous of binding any spirit to a ready obedience to thee, we will shew you how a certain book may be made by which they may be invoked; and this book is to be consecrated a book of Evil Spirits, ceremoniously to be composed in their name and order, whereunto they bind with a certain holy oath, the ready and present obedience of the spirit. This book is therefore to be made of the most pure and clean paper, which is generally called virgin paper; and this book must be inscribed after this manner, viz. let there be drawn on the left side of the book the image of the spirit, and on the right side thereof his character, with the oath above it, containing the name of the spirit, his dignity and place, with his office and power. Yet many magicians do compose this book otherwise, omitting the characters and images; but I think that it is much more efficacious not to neglect any thing above mentioned in the forms.

There is likewise to be observed the circumstances of places, times, hours, according to the stars which these spirits are under, and are seen to agree to; with their site, rite, and order, being applied.

Which book being so written, is to be well bound, adorned, garnished, embellished and kept secure, with registers and seals, lest it should happen after the consecration to open in some part not designed, and endanger the operator. And, above all, let this book be kept as pure and reverent as possible; for irreverance of mind causes it to lose its virtue by pollution and prophanation.

Now this sacred book being thus composed according to the form and manner we have delivered, we are to consecrate it after a two-fold way; the first is, that all and singularly each of the spirits who are written in the book be called to the circle, according to the rites magical, which we have before taught, and place the book which is to be consecrated in a triangle on the outside of the circle; then read, in the presence of the spirits, all the oaths which are contained and written in that book; then the book to be consecrated being already placed without the circle in a triangle there drawn, compel all the spirits to impose their hands where their images and characters are drawn, and to confirm and consecrate the same with a special and common oath. This being done, let the book be shut and preserved as we have spoken before; then licence the spirits to depart according to due rite and magical order.

There is another method extant among us of consecrating a general book of spirits which is more easy, and of as much efficacy to produce every effect, except that in opening this book, the spirits do not always appear visible. And this way is thus: let be made a book of spirits, as we have before shewn, but in the end thereof write invocations, bonds, and strong conjurations, wherewith every spirit may be bound; then bind this book between two lamens or tables, and on the inside thereof draw or let be drawn two holy pentacles of the divine Majesty, which we have before set forth, out of the Apocalypse. Then let the first of them be placed in the beginning, of the book, and the second at the end of the same.

This book being thus perfected, let it be brought, in a clear and fair night, to a circle prepared in a cross-way, according to the art which we have before delivered; and there, in the first place, the book is to be opened, and to be consecrated according to the rites and ways which we have before delivered concerning consecration, which being done, let all the spirits be called which are written in the book, in their own order and place, conjuring them thrice by the bonds described in the book that they come to that place within the space of three days, to assure their obedience and confirm the same, to the book so to be consecrated; then let the book be wrapped up in a clean linen cloth, and bury it in the midst of the circle, and stop the hole so as it may not be perceived or discovered: the circle being destroyed after you have licensed the spirits, depart before sun-rise; and on the third day, about the middle of the night, return and make the circle anew and on thy knees make prayer unto God, and give thanks to him; and let a precious perfume be made, open the hole in which you buried your book and take it out, and so let it be kept, not opening the same. Then after licensing the spirits in their, order and destroying the circle, depart before sunrise. And this is the last rite and manner of consecrating, profitable to whatever writings, experiments, &c. that direct the spirits, placing the same between two holy lamens or pentacles, as is before mentioned.

But when the operator would work by the book thus consecrated he should do it in a fair and clear season, when the spirits are least troubled; and let him turn himself towards the region of the spirits; then let him open the book under a due register, and likewise invoke the spirits by their oaths there described and confirmed, and by the name of their character and image, to whatever purpose you desire, and if there be need conjure them by the bonds placed in the end of the book. And having attained thy desired effect license them to depart.

NEW FOREWORD TO THE ENGLISH EDITION

BY STEVE SAVEDOW

The *Liber Spirituum* or *Book of Spirits* is described in various classic grimoire texts, including *The Book of the Sacred Magic of Abra-Melin the Mage, The Key of Solomon The King, Fourth Book of Occult Philosophy* (attributed to Henry Cornelius Agrippa), and perhaps most notably, *The Magus, or Celestial Intelligencer* by Francis Barrett. It is considered a 'magical tool' of the practitioner, to be used as a talisman during acts of 'high magic', specifically for invocation, conjuration, and evocation[1] of the spirits, both those that are considered as 'evil', and also the good spirits which are known as 'divine', or angelic.

I unexpectedly came across this book as an internet listing with basically just the title, publisher, and copyright details. I was somewhat intrigued, as it included four known grimoire titles. Therefore, I originally assumed it must be some kind of a collection, so I took a chance and ordered it sight unseen. The four titles, which are in Italian and Latin, were the *Book of Shadows, Book of Spirits, True Divine Grimoire*, and *Key of Secrets*. The names 'Book of Shadows' and 'Book of Spirits' are basically generic terms of a particular style of grimoire text.

The *Book of Shadows* (*Liber Umbrarum, Libro Delle Ombre*) generally refers to an aspect of the modern witchcraft revival, whereas a witch compiles a diary of their own workings, original spells, and records of their practices; in other words, it is a personal documentation. The first publication of a book of shadows was compiled by Gerald Gardner, the father of the modern Wicca movement.

> According to Gardner, the rituals and wisdom of the ancient witch cult had survived – only just – thanks to their being recorded in a grimoire known as the *Book of Shadows*. Copies were passed down through covens from one generation to the next. The nature of this grimoire began to be revealed by Gardner, who had received his own copy after his initiation, and was subsequently developed with input from one of his first followers Doreen Valiente, who would later provide a thoughtful self-reflexive history of the movement. Although pirated versions of the *Book of Shadows* began to appear in print from the 1960's onwards, Gardner had produced a manuscript version in the late 1940s entitled *Ye Bok of ye*

---

[1] Translator's note (TN): These terms are often interchangeable depending on the text referenced; however, it has been my experience that 'invocation' is the calling down of the specific energy related to a particular spirit or 'divine' entity; 'conjuration' is the speaking of the actual words of a ritual; and lastly 'evocation' is the summoning of a spirit to visible appearance.

Art Magical. It had the air of a venerable grimoire, with its leather cover, ornate scripts, and spelling mistakes indicative of repeated copying over the generations.²

Additionally, the *Book of Spirits* (*Livre des Esprits, Libro Degli Spiriti, Liber Spirituum*) is a reference to such grimoire texts as the *Goetia* and other 'true' grimoires, which are instructions on how to evoke specific spirits, and which traditionally include a catalogue of demons or spirits. A book of spirits is also known to have been used as a 'magical weapon' during the practice of evocation of some spirits. From *The Goetia of Dr. Rudd*, under the heading 'Binding the Spirit – Ligatio':

> Ligatio is the binding of the spirit with an oath, to an agreement that it will perform the task demanded of it. Ligatio has the secondary meaning of 'to harness'. Ideally the spirit should also 'sign' the Liber Spirituum left open in the Triangle, or mark the seal there drawn in some other unique way.³

This title also brings to mind another important but unrelated text, the *Liber Officiorum Spirituum*, or *Book of the Office of Spirits*, which was a demonological grimoire and a major source for Johann Weyer's *Pseudomonarchia Daemonum* and the *Ars Goetia*. The original work has never been located, but some derived texts bearing the title have been found, some in the Sloane manuscripts, and others in the Folger Shakespeare Library. Each version bears various similarities to the other, though they are far from identical. Johannes Trithemius mentions two separate works (*Liber quoque Officiorum* and *De Officiis Spirituum*), indicating that the text may have branched off by his time.⁴

Another portion of the title is the *Verum Divinum Grimoirum*, being the *True Divine Grimoire*. There is no relationship, however, to the infamous demonological *Grimoirium Verum* or *True Grimoire,* attributed to Alibeck the Egyptian at Memphis and spuriously said to have been translated from the Hebrew by Plaingiere and dated 1517. However, by including the word *divinum*, it implies spirits of divinity such as angels, and in this case, archangels such as Michael, Gabriel and Raphael. The other 'evil spirits' listed in this book, however, are also discussed in *Grimoirium Verum*, although in a different context.⁵

---

2 TN: Davies, 2009:270-271.

3 TN: Skinner & Rankine, 2007:93.

4 TN: See Hockley, 2011; Weyer, 2015-2016; and Weyer, 1991.

5 TN: *Grimorium Verum*, partially translated into English by Arthur Edward Waite, 1898 and reprinted in 1911, also in Shah, 1957. Translated in full by Trident Press (1994), and finally in the most complete and superior version by Joseph Peterson.

Lastly, the final portion of the title is *Clavis Secretorum,* or *Key of the Secrets* (or *Mysteries*). Although there are a few unrelated books with this title, this might possibly be a reference to *Key of the Mysteries*[6] by Eliphas Levi,[7] which reveals the mysteries of religion and the secrets of the Qabalah, providing a sketch of the prophetic theology of numbers. Also, the mysteries of nature, such as spiritualism and fluidic phantoms, are explored and additionally, magical mysteries, the theory of the will with its 22 axioms are divulged. There is also another interesting book by that title, being *Clavis Secretorum* or *Key of Secrets*, attributed to Simon el Mago (Simon the Magus) with chapters on the 'Magic of Solomon', 'Secrets of Hermes Trismegistus', the 'Cabalistic Alphabet', 'Spirits', 'Secrets of Nature', 'Magical Powers', etc.[8]

There is however a definite influence of Eliphas Levi in parts of this book, including the employment of various rituals, specifically the elemental prayers, conjuration of the four, and the qabalistic invocation of Solomon, which are found in the seminal nineteenth century text, *Transcendental Magic.*[9] In addition, as Eliphas Levi famously states in his *History of Magic*:

> The popular traditions of magic affirms that he who possesses the Keys of Solomon can communicate with spirits of all grades and can exact obedience on the part of all natural forces.[10]

There are other subtle hints to Levi herein, for example the initial text of the manuscript section begins with an announcement to the Knights of the Holy Kingdom, or Sanctum Regnum, and continues with three formulas, those of exorcism, conjuration, and consecration, which appear to relate to the *Key of Solomon.*[11]

I was rather pleasantly surprised upon receiving this work. It is an attractive folio size hardcover book bound in striking red sail-cloth with talismanic heavy gilt stamping, pages of quality parchment paper, decorative colored borders and

---

6 TN: First translated to English by Aleister Crowley and published in 1959/1986, also Samuel Weiser, Inc., 2001.

7 TN: Eliphas Lévi Zahed, born Alphonse Louis Constant (1810–1875), was a French estoricist, poet, and author of more than 20 books on magic, Kabbalah, alchemical studies, and occultism. He pursued an ecclesiastical career in the Catholic Church until the age of 26, when he abandoned the priesthood. At the age of 40, he began professing knowledge of the occult, and becoming a reputed ritual magician.

8 TN: *Clavis Secretorum Celis Et Terrae: Recetas Maravillosas Arte Para Volar Y Para Obtener El Fuego Astral*, Etc, 1902.

9 TN: Levi, 1896. Unless otherwise stated, references to Levi, 1896 all refer to *Transcendental Maic* and not *The Magical Ritual of the Sanctum Regnum*.

10 TN: Levi, 1914.

11 TN: See Levi, 1896.

rubrication. It is an original single text with fairly lengthy introductions by both the editor Pier Luca Pierini, who is also the publisher/owner of Edizioni Rebis (an Italian press), as well as by 'Caliel' (Prof. Luigi Petriccione, 1928-1995), who was a Grand Master of Neapolitan Martinism and the Italian Golden Rosicrucian Order. His memorial suggests a direct connection of succession to Eliphas Levi. Mr. Pierini first published the text in 1976, which he had acquired from Caliel, who he claims was his first master in esotericism. The current Italian edition available is noted as the seventh edition, and the latest copyright is from 2013.

There are references (mainly regarding a prayer of ablution) to a periodical text entitled simply *Ur*, which actually refers to a magazine printed in Rome during the years 1927-29 (first, with the title of *Ur*, then later changed to *KRUR*), directed by the scholar Julius Evola and collaborators who were known as Gruppo di Ur, or the Ur Group. In 1955 *Ur* and *KRUR* reunited in three volumes and were printed in Milan by Editori Bocca with the title *Introduzione alla Magia, a cura del Gruppo di Ur*, then afterward, by Edizioni Mediterranee in Rome, as *Introduzione alla Magia quale Scienza dell'Io*, later translated into English as *Introduction to Magic as the Science of the Ego*. Most recently, it has been re-published by Inner Traditions Publishing in 2001, 2019 and 2021, as three paperback volumes.[12] Also mentioned is the name Luce (which translates as 'light'), who was Giulio Parise, a contributor to the original magazine.

It is difficult to add much that is not already covered by the excellent scholarly original introduction offered herein, but in order to provide more context, I wanted to include the following details.

The text is straightforward, with no nonsense, specific, and detailed practical techniques derivative of the classic medieval instructional works. As stated earlier, it draws mainly from the traditional grimoire texts, those being *Book of the Sacred Magic of Abramelin the Mage* (referred to here as the *Arsenal Manuscript*), *Key of Solomon the King*, and additionally incorporating some aspects from *Heptameron or Magical Elements of Peter de Abano*, and *Arbatel De Magia Veterum*.[13] It is most definitely based on sixteenth and seventeenth century magical texts, although apparently it is also influenced by the later writers who copied and re-copied it multiple times, putting down instructions on paper throughout the generations. Also, the original intricate color illustrations of the seven archangels, which are presented for each day of the week to which they are attributed, appear to be taken from the design of the illustration of Cassiel in *The Magus* by Barrett.

In *The Magus* by Barrett, there was a rather specific note mentioned in one of the hand-colored plates which included an artist's rendering of the archangel

---

12 TN: Julius Evola and the Ur Group, 1971, 2001, 2019, 2021.

13 TN: The *Heptameron* and *Arbatel of Magick*, were both originally included in the *Fourth Book Of Occult Philosophy* attributed to Henry Cornelius Agrippa and published in Latin, Marburg: 1554.

Cassiel, with the caption 'Specimen of the Book of Spirits to be Made of Virgin Vellum'. This illustration matches the ones presented here, in the last 15 pages of this book. An interesting bit of bibliographic/antiquarian trivia is that the original edition of 1801 was reprinted in 1875 by Knight and Compton & W. Blackader as an exact reprint of the first edition. It retained the original publication date and publisher's details of the first edition, and it is sometimes mistakenly identified as such. There are, however, a number of minor textual differences, and five of the plates in the reprint edition were colored (there were four usually in the first edition). It was also printed on a different paper type, and had a leather spine with a gilt stamped design of the angel Cassiel. The fifth plate mentioned here is the one with the archangel Cassiel in the *Book of Spirits*, as noted above.

This text dictates a fairly complicated system of high magic, fully outlined and interpreted, starting with preparatory rituals after beginning the New Moon Rite, which is to be performed monthly during the first sixty minutes after every new moon, for six months immediately following the spring equinox, and including daily rites. The instructions include preparations for the temple, called 'the Oratory', daily prayers, clothing, and diet, as well as the rules of daily life and specific directions for three groups of two lunar cycles. This all leads to the ritual of initiation or self-consecration, with detailed rules to be observed for the rest of your life. It also includes construction of the magic circle, and preparation of the robe, altar, sword, pentacle, and wand which are to be used during the rituals.

After the ritual of self-consecration, the magician is now prepared for the Great Operation: rituals to be performed to conjure and contact the higher spirits, including one's personal Holy Guardian Angel, known as the HGA in some modern traditions. This is also known as the summoning of the 'elevated spirit' or the high Geni, which may or may not require a sensitive person to be used as a medium, suggesting either a woman or child to be placed in a hypnotic state,[14] and all this prior to the Great Operation for the Acquisition of Power Over the Princes of the Elements, and the Hostile Elementals, or 'evil spirits'. Finally, it includes instructions on to prepare for the series of seven daily rituals as invocations to the archangels, all of which have various attributes based on astrological planetary aspects. Lastly, everything described here must be fully recorded and detailed in the operator's own personal Book of Shadows.

It is noted from the section on the Great Operation that 'They will therefore begin with the evocation of their own geni, or Guardian Angel, to have self-consecration confirmed, and to receive the amount necessary to evoke them; and to ask them for assistance of all future operations' and then to call upon the elemental and familiar spirits, to teach the practitioner on matters of the magical art, and other various subjects.

The text presented is obviously modernized but has apparently been taken from those classic medieval grimoires, as previously discussed. There have obviously been influences from those students who previously possessed the work, as it is said to have been passed down and copied by hand repeatedly. The 'Historical Introduction' opens by explaining that this text is "always being circulated in manuscript (form), only among the most circumspect and reserved members of an ancient, strictly closed magical brotherhood."[15] The particular magical order noted here is described as being of the Rosicrucian tradition in origin.[16]

Also, in the introduction to the *Book of Abramelin* (page xlvii), MacGregor Mathers quotes from the *Key of Solomon* (Book II, Chapter XXI.) that there are found other directions for invoking spirits as follows:

---

14 TN: Mathers, 1898, introduction, page xli, entitled Appendix B, 'Employment Of A Child Clairvoyant By Cagliostro'. Note the reference to a hypnotic state which is described in the text as sleep.

15 TN: Most likely being a spurious claim to ancient lineage as is common with magical orders.

16 TN: As stated in the memorial of 'Caliel' following the foreword, being Ordine Martinista Di Rito Napolitano (Martinist Order of the Napolitan Rite) and of the Rose + Cross of Gold.).

Make a small Book containing the Prayers for all the Operation, the Names of the Angels in the form of Litanies, their Seal and Characters; the which being done thou shalt consecrate the same unto God and unto the pure Spirits in the manner following: ...[17]

Additionally of interest here, in *Book of Abramelin,* Second Book, Chapter 4, page 56-57, under the heading 'That the Greater Number of Magical Books are False and Vain', MacGregor Mathers states in footnote:

> It is perfectly and utterly true without doubt that Angelic Magic is higher than the form of Talismanic Magic which has its basis in the Astrological positions of the Heavenly Bodies; and can therefore do more, and be also independent of Astrological considerations, because the matter is relegated to a higher plane than this, and one wherein the laws of Physical Nature do not obtain.

The following is taken from the publisher's (Edizioni Rebis) description of this mysterious Italian grimoire:

> Taken from an authentically magical secret manuscript of the Rosicrucian school, the *Book of Shadows* (*Liber Umbrarum*) represents the most powerful and mysterious work that has been published in ceremonial Magic. Numerous testimonies of experimenters who have put into practice the teachings of the work ensure that they have obtained astounding results, sometimes without even following in detail the operations prescribed by the ritual. It is spoken of in all the main treatises on occultism and high magic as a fabulous text, formerly handed down from master to disciple, never published in its full version in the world. For the first time, therefore, an authentic key text of ceremonial magic is offered, the true ancient magic book; the legendary manual of magicians, of which only a few very rare handwritten copies are known; and in which the suggestive forms of the high spirits are illustrated in splendid planetary images; describing the formulas of evocation of the supreme genies and of the elements, their seals, the magic circles, the magic of fire; and the very important unprecedented ceremonies to get in touch with one's own guardian spirit.

---

17 See Appendix B for the complete text of this section.

Purpose

It is safe to assume that (one of) the general purposes of this text is to encourage the practitioner to create their own personal Book of Shadows or Liber Spirituum, in their own particular style, either being an ornate fine leatherbound volume, or simply a three-ring binder or spiral bound notebook. It should be very durable, but mostly it must represent the unique style of the individual magician, of one who is confident and adept as an operator in order to perform the daily rites and acts of high magic that are described herein, and to strictly follow the rules given in their everyday life. It has been my experience that after performing Solomonic evocation, with all the lengthy rituals required for an initial successful evocation of a powerful spirit, including conjuration to visible appearance, and binding them according to the *Lemegeton Clavicula Salomonis* or *Lesser Key of Solomon*,[18] that the act results in a spiritual connection to that spirit, making it somewhat easier to summon them in the future.[19] It is also true that utilizing the Book of Spirits is used to establish a tangible connection to multiple spirits, after having the spirit sign and/or mark the page as described above. This is an example of sympathetic high magic, which generally refers to using a signature, a bit of hair, and sometimes a drop of blood, in order to form a magical connection with a person, for whatever reason. This book appears to suggest that the theory behind sympathetic magic is indeed sound, not only for dealing with humans who are magically involved with the practitioner, but also for the spirits who are meant to be summoned, as well.

As it is known by serious and true practitioners, the key to all ritual magic practice is centred around the grimoires or books of magic, and the techniques outlined therein. This is truly an example of how one's own personal *Book of Shadows* or *Liber Spirituum* should actually appear.

This presentation is an efficient practical system of high magic ritual techniques based on the classical medieval texts, in which the practitioner of the art may conjure and bind multiple spirits specifically to aid and assist them in their daily magical life, and for any task that would be appropriate to employ them. Also, initially and specifically, to acquire your 'holy guardian angel' or elevated spirit, as well as conjuring elemental and familiar spirits, in order to deal with the 'higher spirits' known as the spirit princes and vice princes, and eventually the powerful archangels which are a direct connection to the divine.

As I have suggested in previous writing, after the series of rituals are completed and the various spirits have been successfully summoned along with your HGA, the vice princes, and elemental spirits, the experienced magician should develop their own original system, based on those practices which they have indeed utilized successfully, recording that which has worked for them, and discarding that which

---

18 TN: Peterson, 2001.
19 TN: See Skinner & Rankine, 2007:65.

has not. The practice of ritual magic is difficult in the best of circumstances, for those who are confident and capable of the commitment and dedication to follow these instructions for the initial six months, and to be devoted to them in their daily life.

In closing, it should be made clear that the experienced magician is fully aware that it is considered as an exercise in futility to attempt to combine traditional systems of evocation, i.e.: one should not employ the *Goetia* circle in order to evoke the Olympic spirits of the *Arbatel*. In general, one should never attempt to combine different systems of high magic, as in the best of cases, the operation will be simply prove uneventful, but in the worst of cases, could end up in total disaster. It should be noted however that while the rituals of this book do seem to incorporate the *Key of Solomon*, *Book of Abramelin*, and also *Heptameron of Peter de Abano*, I would suggest that the practitioner do their due diligence in researching the rituals presented here, and employ the appropriate circle based on the specific ritual performed. It should also be made clear that *Abramelin* is one of the only evocational grimoires which does not incorporate a magic circle for protection from the spirits; although it is required here, this is an original design, and is much less complicated than those of the other grimoires mentioned here. The *Liber Spiirituum* is to be placed in the triangle and the spirit conjured is meant to mark the page with its name, sign, and number, so that in the future, the practitioner need only to open the book to the page formerly marked, and then after speaking the appropriate conjuration, the spirit should then appear spontaneously, without all the pomp and circumstance normally required. Typically 'shortcuts' are frowned upon when it comes to ritual magic, however the employment of the *Liber Spiritum* as a Book of Shadows would certainly be an acceptable technique of high magic, having been referenced in the most infamous, important, and reputable texts of the medieval period, therefore it is certain to be a proper and effective method of spirit evocation for those dedicated few with the fortitude to proceed, and to utilize the system and procedures that are detailed herein.

Memorial Biographical Note on 'Caliel'

(Prof. Luigi Petriccione)
by the Ordine Martinista Di Rito Napolitano

Maestro Don Luigi Petriccione (Naples 23-7-1928 - Nozzano S.Pietro 29-3-1995) of the Dukes Giordano d'Oratino, natural son of Eduardo, disciple of 'L'Argonauta'. Among other things, he was Grand Master of Martinism Napolitano and of the Rose + Cross of Gold with the Jeronimi Usarkaf / Caliel, deposits received from the Neapolitan Martinist disciples of Master Eliphas Levi.

 He, among other things, tried to restore an Alliance between the various brotherhoods, orders or existing Friars (of Martinist Rite, Kremmertian, Masonic, Greco-Roman Olympic, etc.), which, despite their respective diversity, are analogical in functions and descend from a single Rose /Cross Aura. He was a distinguished scholar of heraldry and religions. Also in this last field he deepened, in accordance with the R+C doctrine, the fundamental unity of all cults (Christian, Jewish, Islamic, Buddhist, Etruscan, etc. etc.), dating back to a single Primordial Tradition, also called Noachita, Natural Religion, or Prisca Theologia, whose most suitable expression is found in the Universal Apostolic Gnostic Ecclesia. Finally, although he did not deal with profane politics, he was interested in the numerous legends concerning the mythical return of a figure who brings together the royal and priestly power, and who would have the power to restore order in the world. So, Caliel was undoubtedly a very interesting character for the vastness of the fields of knowledge that he penetrated with his conscience.

INTRODUCTORY NOTE TO THE SEVENTH ITALIAN EDITION

BY PIER LUCA PIERINI

We present the seventh reprint[20] of this magical work of great fascination, supplemented by the introductions of a historical, bibliographic and ritual nature, [that were] missing from previous editions. The important added elements make the book complete in all its parts, perfectly conforming to the initial publication project. In this way, even those [who are] interested in the more strictly operational aspects of the *Book of Shadows* (*Liber Umbrarum*) will be able to have a broad and reliable doctrinal guide, combined with a series of valid instructions and detailed, specific teachings, set out with precision; as it hardly appears in most ancient rituals and grimoires, in perfect and rigorous harmony with the fundamental canons of the ceremonial tradition.

We are therefore reasonably convinced that this new edition of the *Divine Grimoire* (*Grimorium Divinum*), [which is] a text that for [more than] thirty years continues to garner the keenest interest and consideration of specialists in the area [of grimoires], will be particularly appreciated by all scholars and researchers who carefully follow our work[21] of enhancing the most precious and representative texts of ancient magic.

---

20 TN: Viareggio: Edizioni Rebis, 2013.
21 TN: The work of Edizioni Rebis, the publisher of numerous occult texts in quality binding.

Historical Introduction to the Fifth Italian Edition

by Pier Luca Pierini

Compared to all the other known grimoires, the *True Divine Grimoire* (*Verum Grimorium Divinum*) appears [to be] the only one authentically and deeply imprinted by a clear form of traditional divine magic; as well as strictly consistent with the doctrines, and fundamental principles of hermetic philosophy.

The text is extremely rare, always being circulated in manuscript [form], only among the most circumspect and reserved members of an ancient, strictly closed magical brotherhood, certainly [related to] Rosicrucianism,[22] if not certainly Rosicrucian,[23] with all certainty still operating in the last century.

A completely fortuitous event allowed us to publish it for the first time under the title of *Book of Shadows* (*Liber Umbrarum*) in a partial edition with many edits, [which] excluded all the detailed secret ritual instructions for its use; in which, by prudential measure some formulas, [were] considered too powerful, and [were] given only in an Italian translation rather than in the original Latin.[24]

The *Grimorium*[25] as it has been disclosed has proved very powerful and effective to more than one practitioner, of those who have wanted to experience it; and its disclosure has not caused any harm or recrimination by anyone. This is why, in this edition, the work is presented in its entirety, with all its ritual instructions, and

---

22 TN: The Order of the Rose Cross. Rosicrucianism is a spiritual and cultural movement, with European roots in the early 17th century.

23 TN: 'Rosa+Croce'.

24 TN: The first edition was published in the mid 1970s.

25 *True Grimoire*, this is not to be confused with the classic demonological *Grimorium Verum*, as described in the foreword, is characterized by a high moral conscience, for which its ceremonies do not aim like those of the ordinary grimoires, nor at concluding 'pacts with the devil', nor at the dominion 'over the beast' for selfish purposes. On the contrary, this work proposes authentic practices of asceticism aimed at contact with elevated spirits and with the geni of science, showing in this way various points of contact with *The Magic of Arbatel*, as with the best *Clavicles of Solomon*, Abramelin's Magic (commonly referred to as the *Arsenal Manuscript*, and Pietro d'Abano's *Heptameron*, to aim only at a later time, when the ties with the Aeons of Light were consolidated, at the dominion over the elementary and malignant spirits, understood as a function of their subjection as analogue to the subjugation of the forces of evil in the state according to the royal art or 'holy of kings' for sacred purposes, making explicit reference, as well as to the figure of King Solomon; who according to tradition, used evil spirits for the construction of the temple, and for other works of the glory of God. Also to the doctrine of 'Apocatastasis', typical of divine magic and revived by Origen, according to which also evil spirits are called to redeem themselves, albeit through the fulfillment, by mere contrition of holy works

with the addition of this [new] Introduction, and some explanatory notes, both by the [original] translator. All the formulas[26] are given this time in full in the original Latin.

The use of the *Grimorium* for this purpose presupposes in the operator a great steadiness and profound righteousness of purpose, full balance and sublime feeling; a vast science and great rigor in behavior as well as a strong attitude to command; combined with an aristocratic style of domination towards the spirits; these things (that it) is not possible to teach, or even outline succinctly in this brief introduction; but which also the modern aspirant to these practices should know well; whereas in the norm, they are much less prepared than the ancient aspirants, to the knowledge of the sacred of their world, and the way to move there.

The reader will be able to find however, in this new edition, the detailed secret instructions, rituals and practices, both on the behavior required of the magician, and on his relations with the entities of light and shadow.

The practices and rites constituting the preparatory asceticism for the acquisition of magical powers are offered with great clarity from their very nature; that is from the tenor of the prayers or from the formulas. It appears with all evidence that it is divinity the aspiring magician asks from the powers; and he will always repeat them once he has obtained them, assuming in the operator, both (that) they acquire that for their conservation, the rectitude of conscience and of work, the honesty of life, and submission to the divine will.

Moreover, even ancient works such as the Arab grimoires[27] used to warn the reader of the certain loss of all power as a consequence of any violation of divine law, which is significantly represented in the symbolic account of the loss of King Solomon's magic ring as a result of his going astray, and the finding of it as a result of his repentance and redemption.[28]

As for the practice, we will observe that our *Grimorium* requires as indispensable, according to current magical customs, a ritual robe of linen or other white vegetable

---

26 TN: The prayers, conjurations and invocations.

27 TN: Arabic grimoires, e.g. *Picatrix* or *Ghāyat al-Ḥakīm*, which most scholars assume was originally written in the middle of the 11th century. Also, *Kitāb al-Bulhān* or *Book of Wonders*, a 14th-15th century Arabic manuscript, the contents include subjects on astronomy, astrology and geomancy, including a section of full-page illustrations.

28 TN: There are a few legends regarding the Ring of Solomon. According to the Talmud, Solomon's ring was engraved with the Shem Hamephoresh, being the Ineffable Name of God. Islamic writers say that it contained 'the Most Great Name of God' along with four jewels that had been given to Solomon by angels. It is said that he lost the ring in the Jordan River, and considered it to be lost forever, until a fisherman later came to him. He had found the ring inside a fish, and returned it to the king.

fibre to be worn in all ceremonies;[29] impeccable moral conduct; being in the grace of God (by) ritual chastity at least in the last two of the six months of preparatory prayers, to be extended up to the full compliment of the Great Operation; the ritual abstention before the same for various lunations[30] from any food coming from dead animals; the diet being reduced in recent times to a single daily meal.[31]

Both the New Moon Rite[32] each month and that of the consecration of the magician, like that of the Great Operation, must be preceded by a complete ritual bath or shower. During the bath, psalms n. 26 'Dominus Illuminatio mea' and n. 13 'Dixit Insipiens in corde di lui' preferably in the original Latin. The Martinists[33] and the Elifaslevian Kabbalists also found the exorcism of water given by Eliphas Levi in chap. IV of his 'Ritual',[34] while other traditionalist currents, which make use of a special circle of which the figure is given below, have experimented with satisfaction [using] the formula 'For ablution', given by Luce in chap. XI of *Ur*, vol. I, others [make use] of the Latin formula: 'Ut aqua lavat petram, sic purificetur corpus phisicum meum per actionem manus meae ab omnibus cupiditatibus, passionibus et praevaricationibus et corpus subtile meum ab omnibus malis influxibus absorptis'.[35]

Another point left rather vague, both in this as in other grimoires, but of fundamental importance, is that the common man, and especially the one gifted for the practice of magic (which is not to be confused with clairvoyance and sensitivity), alone except in exceptional and very rare cases can hardly contact the evoked entities directly, neither audibly nor visually.

In order to communicate with them, that is, to receive and perceive their answers, the operator who is not naturally sensitive or visionary must use a psychic or a psychic in ecstasy, or in a lucid state, as it is said today, who is placed in the circle in a comfortable chair with armrests, or lying on the ground, and can report

---

29 It will be good to have the embroideries provided by the Clavicles of Solomon 1750 (republished in full by Edizioni Rebis), with the (other) *Grimorium* works and is in close relationship.
TN: the 1750 edition of *Key of Solomon* is generally equated with *La Veritable Magie Noire* (*True Black Magic*), which was only recently translated to English by Joseph Peterson in 2017. See Peterson 2017:182-84. Additionally, see *Abramelin*, Second Book, in the 9th, 11th and 12th Chapter.

30 TN: Lunar cycle.

31 TN: There are also specific requirements in regards to clothing, diet and fasting in *Abramelin*, pp xlvi-xlvii, also in various sections of the Second Book.

32 TN: The Neomenial Rite.

33 TN: A form of esoteric Christianity.

34 TN: Part 2 of Levi, 1896:187-411. Chapter IV:231 is the Exorcism of Water.

35 TN: 'As water washes the rock, so my physical body is purified by the action of my hand from all desires, passions, and transgressions, and my subtle body absorbed by all evil influences.'

precisely. Otherwise, in the most fortunate of hypotheses, the operator will hear only untranslatable blows on the walls, as can be confirmed by all those who tried without the help of a sensitive [medium].

As far as the consecration of the magician is concerned, this should be officiated by a master of the hermetic tradition, to whom the ritual of our grimoire belongs. On the basis of this rule, the aspirant who was not in contact with any master of this tradition, would remain unappealable and excluded from the consecration and practice of magic. On the other hand, there are cases of self-consecration for rites only, that is, cases in which it is possible to connect to the Chain Egregore[36] of a distant, or even extinct brotherhood. Among others we will remember that the *Arsenal Manuscript*, in Book II chap. XII,[37] it teaches in detail 'How one must consecrate oneself in order to work well'. The rite is very similar to that of our *Grimorium*, so at least in certain cases, an independent consecration from uninterrupted and direct initiatory affiliation is possible. The *Grimorium* also gives the rules for the transmission of magical powers to disciples of the self-consecrated magician, and therefore for the resumption of the initiatory line of succession.

This concerns practical use of the *Grimorium*.

As for its origins, its dating, and its authorship, we must say that, as for most of the most ancient magical texts, it is very difficult to trace the exact sources.[38] The style of the operation seems quite uniform, which makes us lean towards the hypothesis of a homogeneous work, [that is] the work of a single author, even if there are numerous similarities with other ancient grimoires, and entire formulas identical to those in *Arbatel* or the *Clavicles*, or the *Book of Abramelin* and to book of Pietro d'Abano, which are found more or less in all the white grimoires in an almost identical form, without being able to prove the derivation from one or on the other hand, with the exception of the works of Pietro d'Abano, who being the oldest author, [had] influenced the following grimoires.

---

36 TN: An egregore is a group thought-form. It can be created either intentionally or unintentionally, and becomes an autonomous entity with the power to influence.

37 P.113 et seq. Of the French edition edited by Ambelain, at Niclaus (the Italian translation is present in the work *Magia Segreta* volume III, Edizioni Rebis.
TN: Mathers 1898:77, 'How One Should Keep Oneself In Order To Carry Out This Operation Well'.

38 TN: It appears to me that this actual book dates back at least to the 19th century, based on the manner of writing, and also the Latin portions also appear to be contemporary rather than medieval. This time frame matches also if we consider the influence of Eliphas Levi, who passed away in 1875. This is not to suggest that the text of the manuscript is not drawn from ancient sources, as the manuscript is said to have been copied repeatedly and passed from generation to generation.

Regarding d'Abano, we know with certainty how his work must be placed in the Byzantine cultural area,[39] from which the influence of all Middle Eastern magic, [including] Greek, Jewish and Arab, reaches him. In fact, in the rituals of this author we encounter Greek words of power (rhemata),[40] mixed with Jewish and Arabic Shem-Hamphorash,[41] which is typical of middle-eastern magic, in which very ancient Babylonian and Egyptian sources converge, up to the most recent Gnostic and hermetic sources.

Our *Grimorium*, certainly later than d'Abano, from which it draws various formulas, was however entirely written, as it seems, by a single author, who also drew on numerous other medieval sources, (either) Christian or Christianized. The frequent mentions of the Virgin Mary in the text, indeed demonstrates the absolute Catholic inspiration of the work, perfectly in order with the theology, both patristic and scholastic; which makes us suppose that the author of the work was a Catholic priest or bishop, or in any case preceding the western schism.

A significant characteristic of the work that we are considering, and which it has in common only with the *Arbatel*[42] and the *Arsenal Manuscript*, is the request to the divinity for a Divine Spirit, once again referred to as the complementary of the aspirant, who teaches him the magic science and the rules of its use. Such a demand is completely lacking in the *Clavicle* as in the other white grimoires. We do not speak of the blacks[43] like that of Honorius, and others. The words used in our *Grimorium* are indeed the same that *Arbatel* uses to ask the same thing; but how (do we) establish the priority of one or the other texts?

Even if in the editing, we have (that) so far the Latin style of the *Divine Grimoire* (*Grimorium Divinum*) seems to be classifiable as dating back to the Renaissance, taking into account the fact already noted, that some formulas are much older than this work, to which the current drafting constitutes a point of arrival (which is) after the continuous alterations and updates that are recognized there; and which moreover, are a usual fact for ancient copyists, who used to introduce glosses and manipulations rom every rewrite, or omit passages from them (as being)

---

39 TN: The Byzantine Empire, also referred to as the Eastern Roman Empire or Byzantium, was the continuation of the Roman Empire in its eastern provinces during Late Antiquity and the Middle Ages, when its capital city was Constantinople.

40 TN: Rhema ῥῆμα in Greek, literally means an 'utterance' or 'thing said'. It is a word that signifies the action of utterance. In philosophy, it was used by both Plato and Aristotle to refer to propositions or sentences. <https://en.wikipedia.org/wiki/Rhema>

41 TN: Shem HaMephorash – שם המפורש – (alternatively Shem ha-Mephorash or Schemhamphoras), meaning 'the explicit name', is an originally Tannaitic term, describing a hidden name of God in Kabbalah (including Christian and Hermetic variants), and in some more mainstream Jewish discourses. It is composed of either 4, 12, 22, 42, or 72 letters (or triads of letters), the latter version being the most common.

42 TN: Aphorisms 26 & 27.

43 TN: Black magic grimoires like the *Grimoire of Pope Honorius*.

discounted or outdated; the ritual as such and to be considered in its substance very ancient and of the Hellenistic age,[44] despite its current drafting, cannot be placed further back than to the Renaissance.

Hellenistic, Gnostic and hermetic are in fact the words of power that are encountered in the text, clearly recognizable despite the numerous transliterations undergone in the course of translations from one language to another.

Moreover, a typical characteristic of the Babylonian and Egyptian magical formulas, as of the Hebrew and Arabic – a characteristic almost forgotten or (at the least) weakened in the Latin grimoires of the Middle Ages – is found here instead very marked of the formulas, in asking for a favor from the divinity, to cite one or more mythical cases of exemplary power of granting the grace itself; and they insist on extending the structures of the event to the personal case of the praying person, which metastorically[45] is also placed in mythical time and identified in the conclusion, that is, in the positive result to achieve with the ritual, with the mythical case or cases mentioned.

Such a technique, well known in the modern history of religions,[46] is clearly described in the fourth book of the *De Occulta Philosophia* of Pseudo-Agrippa, which dates back to no later than the Renaissance, but which is found only in our *Grimorium*, where it appears with all the Egyptian-Jewish structural characteristics.

Well, this return to style as well as to the Egyptian-Jewish sources of magic, is characteristic of Renaissance hermeticism; and even more of that manifestation known as the R+C of Germany, which in hermeticism accentuates the characteristics of Christian esotericism.

On the other hand, the effectiveness of a grimoire does not depend so much on its antiquity, as on the power of the tradition to which it belongs. We know that our *Grimorium* comes with all evidence, from the still living and powerful hermetic tradition, in its Christian-Kabbalistic form proper to the Rose+Cross. From the ritual point of view, it appears indeed as the purest and most complete manifestation of this tradition.

A further characteristic identifies the *Grimorium* as typically Rosicrucian: the harmonious synthesis of Christian-Catholic theological conceptions, with practical customs. Rites and formulas of the hermetic and Hebrew-Kabbalistic Tradition, a synthesis that allows us to place their origin in time with a good approximation, at least as regards the editing we have, not before the implementation of the kabbalah in the hermetic tradition; acknowledgment that must be traced back to Giovanni

---

44 TN: The Hellenistic period spans the period of Mediterranean history between the death of Alexander the Great in 323 BCE and the emergence of the Roman Empire, as signified by the Battle of Actium in 31 BCE and the conquest of Ptolemaic Egypt the following year.

45 TN: metastoricamente.

46 TN: Eliade, 1979/1981; Van Der Leeuw, 1933; Hubert & Marcel Mauss, 1999.

Reuchlin, (1455-1522);[47] or at the latest, to Pico della Mirandola (1463-1494).[48]

If the Latin of the text had been more elegant and easy, we might have risked the name of Marsilio Ficino;[49] but in the current state of affairs, both for stylistic reasons concerning Latin, and for graphic reasons concerning Hebrew, which is very well transliterated and transcribed; we prefer to hypothesize that the *Grimorium* was compiled in the cosmopolitan and very composite, but very learned, environment of the Hermetic Court of Rudolph II of Habsburg;[50] that is, in the environment of the golden R+C of Germany at the end of the 16th century; as after all, it indicates the date marked on the title page (which is) 1573, a date which we therefore consider to be good,[51] as referring to the drafting of the manual in its current form.

Furthermore, with reference to what we have observed above, regarding the request for 'a spirit that teaches magic' to the operator, a characteristic that is encountered only in the *Arbatel*[52] and in the *Arsenal Manuscript*, as well as in our *Grimorium*; we (make) note that this request presupposes the profession of a conception of magic; which in certain cases is independent of belonging to an initiatory transmission chain in the visible, based on the figure of the Invisible or inner master, who appears in occultism precisely with the Rose+Cross; and who it will degenerate into the guiding spirit of spiritism.

It is precisely this character that confirms once again the Rosa+Croce origin of our *Grimorium*, in addition to those already noted; and in particular,

---

47 TN: Johann Reuchlin was a German Catholic humanist and a scholar of Greek and Hebrew, whose work also took him to modern-day Austria, Switzerland, and Italy and France.

48 TN: Giovanni Pico della Mirandola was an Italian Renaissance nobleman and philosopher. He is famed for the events of 1486, when, at the age of 23, he wrote the Oration on the Dignity of Man, which has been called the 'Manifesto of the Renaissance', and a key text of Renaissance humanism, and of what has been called the 'Hermetic Reformation'. He was the founder of the tradition of Christian Kabbalah, a key tenet of early modern Western esotericism.

49 TN: Marsilio Ficino (1433 –1499) was an Italian scholar and Catholic priest who was one of the most influential humanist philosophers of the early Italian Renaissance. He was an astrologer, a reviver of Neoplatonism in touch with the major academics of his day, and the first translator of Plato's complete extant works into Latin.

50 TN: Rudolph II (or Rudolph the Kind) (1552-1612) was Count of Habsburg in the Aargau (in Switzerland) and a progenitor of the royal House of Habsburg.

51 TN: It was common practice for writers or composers of the classic grimoire texts to note much earlier dates from their actual publication, e.g *Le Dragon Rouge* is dated 1521 when it was actually published about three centuries later, and the earliest *Abramelin* text (which is referenced here) claims the date of 1458, when it has recently been established to be from 1608.

52 TN: See *Arbatel*, Aphorism 13, 'And if you ask for it, one will be given to you, who will teach you what your soul desires, regarding the nature of things.'

its conformity to the liturgy, theology and Christian-Catholic ethics which are proper to the R+C (in preference to the Jewish liturgy which is that of the *Arsenal Manuscript*, also characterized by the presence of the invisible master); the religion of this brotherhood, apart from certain reformist intemperances of the Fama Fraternitatis[53] and the Manifesto of R+C in Paris , being the Catholic one from its origins dating back to the first Hungarian Court of Matthias Corvinus,[54] and then to the Hapsburg Court of Rudolph I, up to the thirteenth century with 'Sincerus Renatus', the Catholic priest Samuel Richter,[55] and up to his most recent events.

Further significant in this regard is the presence, in the formula of consecration of the magus provided by the *Grimorium*; of expressions and of entire passages belonging to the royal consecration rituals of the Catholic Church,[56] formulas dating back to the Middle Ages, which are common both to the Capetian Monarchy[57] and to the Germanic Empire, at the top of which the R+C flowers. And as a further confirmation of all this, note the initial address of the Grimoire, addressed to the 'Knights of the Holy Kingdom', and the reference, in the text of the 'Great Invocation' to the 'Holy Empire appointed by God to the whole earth', in place of what all the other white grimoires usually do 'to the Church and its Sacraments'.[58]

---

53 TN: *Fama fraternitatis Roseae Crucis oder Die Bruderschaft des Ordens der Rosenkreuzer*, usually listed as *Fama Fraternitatis Rosae Crucis*, is an anonymous Rosicrucian manifesto published in 1614 in Kassel, Hesse-Kassel (in present-day Germany). In 1652, Thomas Vaughan translated the work into English. An Italian edition was published as an appendix of the 77th Advertisement (part), under the title *Generale Riforma dell' Universo* (Universal Reformation of Mankind), from a German translation of Bocallini's *Ragguagli di Parnasso* (Advertisements from Parnassus). The *Fama* was soon published in separate form.

54 TN: Matthias Corvinus (1443–1490), was King of Hungary and Croatia from 1458 to 1490.

55 TN: In 1710, Sigmund Richter, founder of the secret society of the Golden and Rosy Cross, also suggested the Rosicrucians had migrated eastward. In the first half of the 20th century, René Guénon, a researcher of the occult, presented this same idea in some of his works.

56 J. Pierre Bayard, *Le Sacre des Rois*, ed. La Columbe, Paris, passini.

57 TN: The Capetian dynasty, also known as the House of France, is a dynasty of Frankish origin, and a branch of the Robertians. It is among the largest and oldest royal houses in Europe and the world, and consists of Hugh Capet, the founder of the dynasty, and his male-line descendants, who ruled in France without interruption from 987 to 1792, and again from 1814 to 1848. The senior line ruled in France as the House of Capet from the election of Hugh Capet in 987 until the death of Charles IV in 1328. That line was succeeded by cadet branches, the Houses of Valois and then Bourbon, which ruled without interruption until the French Revolution abolished the monarchy in 1792. The Bourbons were restored in 1814 in the aftermath of Napoleon's defeat, but had to vacate the throne again in 1830 in favor of the last Capetian monarch of France, Louis Philippe I, who belonged to the House of Orléans.

58 Compare d'Abano *Heptameron* and Solomon *Le Clavicole*, Rebis editions.

The distinctly Ghibelline[59] formula of the Great Invocation, combined with that of the initial address, is an undeniable manifestation of the German Rose+Cross, governed by its Imperator as an esoteric form of the Holy Empire represented as 'Synarchy'.[60] So everything leads us back to Rudolph II.

---

59 TN: The Guelphs and Ghibelline were factions supporting the Pope and the Holy Roman Emperor, respectively, in the Italian city-states of Central Italy and Northern Italy. During the 12th and 13th centuries, rivalry between these two parties formed a particularly important aspect of the internal politics of medieval Italy. The struggle for power between the Papacy and the Holy Roman Empire arose with the Investiture Controversy, which began in 1075, and ended with the Concordat of Worms in 1122.

60 'Sinarchia'. Synarchism generally means 'joint rule' or 'harmonious rule'. The word synarchy is used, especially among French and Spanish speakers, to describe a shadow government or deep state, a form of government where political power effectively rests with a secret elite, in contrast to an oligarchy where the elite is or could be known by the public.

TRUE DIVINE GRIMOIRE (VERUM GRIMORIUM DIVINUM) BOOK OF SHADOWS (LIBER UMBRARUM)

Ritual Instructions and Practical Use.
Collected, sorted and exposed.
Edited by Caliel (Prof. Luigi Petriccione), Naples, 1958.

Ritual instructions and Rules of Use

The ritual instructions are transcribed [here] in full, for operators of good will. Those who can follow them, do so by strictly adhering to what is indicated. Those who do not have the opportunity of observing them entirely should limit themselves to the essential points, realizing what is prescribed to the best of their abilities.

At least six months before starting the series of operations of this rite, we will devote ourselves to studying and meditating well on these instructions, which we must know and possess to perfection.

The maximum age limit traditionally indicated to start the execution of this rite expires at the age of fifty; however, for those who practice or have already practiced ceremonial magic, and therefore possess adequate experience, the limit is raised to sixty-five years.[61]

For those who no longer have the intention or the awareness of wanting and being able to perform the rite until its conclusion, or at least until the evocation of their geni or guardian angel, it is much better that they don't even [attempt to] undertake it.

However, [the operator] not fear having to interrupt the rite due to a major force or for unforeseeable reasons, since in this case, no one would blame them.

If, once you start the operations, some small indisposition should occur, try to carry out both the New Moon Rite and the daily one equally; the latter [should be performed] even less [often] in the morning hours than usual.

---

61 TN: Mathers 1897, in the Second Book, third chapter, titled 'Of The Age And Quality Of The Person Who Wisheth To Undertake This Operation', it notes 'his age ought not to be less than twenty five years nor more than fifty.'

If however, the illness were to worsen so as to require remedies, or worse, if a bloodletting[62] becomes necessary, it being imperatively prescribed that for all the moons of the duration of the preparatory rite, and also of the Great Operation, we must avoid losing blood, except for what may come out due to spontaneous hemorrhage, that is without trauma; do not insist on continuing the rite against the will of divine providence.

We give up temporarily by ending (the operations) with a short prayer, in which we thank God for having warned us in this way, to interrupt (it) for our good.

After the healing, and at the right time, the rite can be restarted from the beginning.

If on the other hand, the operations are interrupted by whim or lightness, or carelessness, or laziness, or other (issues), (then they should) never think about it again; the interrupted rites (will) produce the exact opposite effect to that originally intended.

Instructions Relating to the Entire Duration of the Rite

The entire series of preparatory operations lasts six months (lunations), divided into three group of two each.

It is necessary to have prepared a new sword, (with) the classic ceremonial or cross-shaped hand guard; (it is) better if the sword is twisted and garnished with two moons, the horns turned outwards at the ends of the handguard,[63] a white linen robe, the ritual handwritten by the practitioner, with the formulas of the prayers and conjurations of the rite.

Everything will first be exorcised, then averted[64] and finally blessed.[65]

It will begin on the new moon immediately following the spring equinox, or in another lunation that begins on Sunday; which means, since the rite must last at least six months, so that if this lunation is not of Libra, the rite will be extended by as many moons, so (that) the chosen moon precedes (either) Aries or Libra.

---

62 TN: The medical practice of 'bloodletting' was utilized until about the mid 19th century, when physicians conducted studies that showed that it wasn't effective. It was previously believed to rid the body of impure fluids to cure a variety of conditions. Originally, bloodletting involved cutting a vein or artery (typically at the elbow or knee) to remove the affected blood.

63 TN: See the diagram of the sword in the section 'Formula of Consecration' in the manuscript section, on page 44 of the Italian edition. Also, in Mathers, 1889, Book 1, plate xiv.

64 TN: 'scongiurato' or 'charmed'.

65 Excellent clavicle formulas and those of Piobb *Formulaire de Haute Magie* Dangles, Paris. French edition.
TN: i.e. *Key of Solomon* and Piobb, 1937.

In the additional moons, it will operate as in the first two.

The aspirant to this magic of fire will have previously installed them in a house, where they are sheltered from the gaze of anyone, therefore (it is) better in the countryside.

But if the house is in the city, at least there (should be) a garden enclosed by a high wall, (so that) no one can see the oratory intended for the rites, through the open window.[66]

Both Christians and Jews will be wary of any servile work in the feasts commanded by their respective religions.

All six lunations will be absolutely guarded against contact with any dead body, corpse or carrion, even of freshly killed animals (meant) to be eaten.

The cleaning of the oratory - a room specially used for operations that will symbolically assume the image and function of the temple - will take place every day, early in the morning where possible, and no later than sunset, or at least (done) on Monday and Friday.

It must always be kept neat and clean, having to reflect the purity of the aspirant, and of their work.

NEW MOON RITE[67]

It will begin with the New Moon Rite which must be performed once a month, in the hour between the moment of the phase of the new moon, and the following 60 minutes, regardless of the daily rite.

If at the first lunation, the phase should fall after the hour of the morning rite, (then it) will be moved to immediately after the New Moon Rite, and carried out after it.

After having washed with a full bath or shower, during which the formulas of use are recited,[68] for the traditionalists the formula: 'Numen[69] of the deep sea', given by Luce of UR, vol. I, chap XI;[70] for Christians and Jews, the Psalms 26 (Dominus Illuminatio mea), and 13 (Dixit insipiens in corde suo). The aspirant, dressed in new clothes or white linen, will enter the oratory previously intended for the operations of this rite; and equipped with an oil lamp, a perfume (incense) burner and a lectern, or of an altar; a few minutes after the astronomical moment

---

66 TN: Compare with the *Abramelin* instructions as to the Oratory.

67 TN: The Neomenial Rite.

68 These are for the Martinists, the Formulas of the Exorcism of Water. *Dogma and Ritual* of Eliphas Levi, Ch. IV.
TN: See 1896:231 'Exorcism of the Water', also in Appendix A.

69 TN: 'Numen' meaning 'God' or 'divinity' (Latin).

70 TN: 1971:325, describing the ablution prayer as noted earlier.

of the phase (local time), and never before.[71]

1) They trace the circle which figures are given in its place, facing east, on any day and at any time the phase falls.[72]

2) When the lamp is lit (which can be replaced by two white candles), and the royal incense is thrown on the embers of the perfume burner;[73] they will recite after entering the circle (always facing east), and after having been marked according to the religion or the tradition belonging (optional).

3) Psalms 132 and 133;[74] or, alternatively to them, the Qabalistic invocation of Solomon (Eliphas Levi, *Ritual*, chap. XIII)[75] followed by the 'Prayer of the Salamanders' in the spring, of the Sylphs, of the Undines and of the Gnomes[76] in the successive seasons in the order (Chap. IV); we will then say a short prayer.

4) Prayer for the Hermetic Tradition.

On the day of the New Moon, from the very first lunation, starting from the moment of the phase, the aspirant to the magic of fire will observe a partial fast of 24 hours, during which only one meal is allowed; of which there will be no food from dead animals (neither meat, nor fish, nor animal margarine, nor lard, etc.
Let the rest of the combustion of the perfume [incense] from this rite and in the following ones, both the New Moon Rite and the daily, never be scattered or thrown in the garbage, but buried in a clean place, such as a garden, forest, etc.

---

71 TN: This is quite different from the 'Exorcism of the Water' presented in Mathers, 1889, Book Two, Chapter V.

72 The circle is drawn with chalk or charcoal, and the prayers given in the *Grimorium* are to be recited (while) doing so.
TN: Also, see Mathers, 1889, Book One, Chapter III for 'Construction of the Circle', and Book Two, Chapter IX, for 'Formation of the Circle'.

73 TN: E.g. making the cross on your forehead, if Catholic. Additionally, there is no recipe in the text for the incense or oil to be used, but it would be lofical to assume that the incense and oil described in *Abramelin* and *Key of Solomon* is satisfactory, as, according to Mr. Pierini, 'Royal Incense corresponds to pure incense. The Abramelin recipe may be fine for the oil, as well as for the incense from the Keys of Solomon, provided there are no references to animal sacrifice (pigeon blood or similar).'

74 Prayers and Conjurations are to be recited in a normal voice, from the heart and without hesitation.

75 TN: Levi 1896:297. Also, see Appendix A.

76 TN: Salamanders: fire, spring, east; Sylphs: air, summer, south; Undines: water, autumn, west; Gnomes: earth, winter, north. See 1896:229-232. Also, these four prayers are presented in Appendix A.

Daily Rites

1) For the daily rites, having made the ablutions, which can be simplified and reduced to the face, hands, and sexual parts, the practitioner, dressed in new clothes of white linen, will enter the oratory a few minutes after the astronomical sunrise; and open the window after lighting the lamp, and burning some incense, tracing the circle oriented according to the time,[77] will enter it always facing the direction of the circle, having marked it according to the observed tradition, to the right at the top, and [with] palm open, fingers outstretched, read:

2) Reading of the Holy *Book of Judges* 13:15-23, after which they put more incense on the embers, and recite:

3) The Prayer of Request, given in the *Grimorium*, followed by:

4) Conjuration of the angel of the day (and only of the angel of that day).[78]

Each of these conjurations ends with a request or petition addressed to the angel, which is always the same every day.

1) Petition or request, formula given in the *Grimorium*.

2) To mark oneself according to the observed tradition.

3) Sprinkle water and blessed salt in the four directions, and exit the circle.

Once the rite has been recited, the window will be closed and the oratory will be left; it will remain well closed to prevent strangers from entering. The same operator will no longer enter until sunset, for the sunset rite, [which is] identical to that of the morning, except for the orientation of the circle, and therefore the direction towards which one operates, which will now be towards the west.

If for the new moons following the first, the hour of the [lunar] phase falls after that of the Matins Rite, this is postponed until after the New Moon Rite.

The oratory is often washed with running water, and no one enters it, except for the same operator (alone).

The room will also always be well scented with incense, and well cleaned.

The operator will always be able to sleep with their wife or partner in the first

---

[77] Towards the east for the Matins Rite; towards the west for the Sunset Rite, and when it occurs, towards the south, for the Noon Rite.

[78] TN: See the seven archangels for the days of the week, matching those in the *Heptameron* (and also *The Magus* by Barrett), and their invocations are presented at the end of this book.

two lunations of the rite, except in the days of their monthly rules,[79] up to 24 hours after the return to normal.

On the next four moons, intercourse is avoided.

Every Saturday, the bed sheets and all linen will be changed.

On Sundays, the room will be regularly perfumed with fumigations of incense, or aromatic herbs.

A complete bath, or at least complete ablutions for the whole body, is mandatory on Mondays and Fridays, with the formulas for use.

Whoever can free themself from work commitments should do so.

During the day, after lunch, passages from sacred or initiatory texts will be read for two hours.

The reading of appropriate psalms at least twice a week is to be considered useful.

You will avoid the game[80] like the plague because it is the cause of alteration.

Whoever has weaknesses or had the habit of some vice or harmful forms of addiction, should free themselves from it under pain of getting nowhere; we will always behave in the best possible way.

During the whole period of the six lunations, you can be sure that you will be subjected by the adverse forces to all kinds of temptations, above all to that of prevarication, to abandon the rite; and states of anguish of great restlessness about the success.

All these temptations must be resisted tirelessly.[81]

Whatever religion the aspirant belongs to, they can observe the festivities [which are] not in contrast with the execution of the rite, unless the celebrations of the feasts involve a violation of the diet prescribed for it; such violations must be avoided.

With regard to behaviour, a firm and sincere resolution should be made to correct all errors which, in careful examinations of conscience, one will discover that one [has] committed, and that they firmly undertake to seriously study and overcome it.

Avoid profane futile conversation, especially with people unrelated to magic.

Avoid getting irritated for any reason, and eat and drink sparingly.

It is allowed to go back to sleep after the Morning Prayer.

Whoever does not get up by chance and involuntary on time for the morning rite, can exceptionally officiate it later, but do not abuse this possibility. The prayer is much more effective if done at the proper time.

In the first months of the operations, it will be possible to practice therapeutic

---

79 TN: i.e. menses.

80 TN: Gambling.

81 TN: See Mathers, 1898, Second Book, 20th Chapter, for similar rules of how to live your life in purity and goodness.

magic, and all works of mercy towards the neighbour (only in the first four moons); and one must always abstain from any act of evil magic.

In the last two moons, it is also necessary to abandon therapeutic magic and charity, in order to deal only with spiritual and divine matters.

Special instructions for the Three Groups of Lunations

In the first two lunations:

There are no particular obligations to be respected in addition to those already given for all lunations.

In the second two lunations:

The rite will be officiated in the morning and at sunset in the forms given above, but from the evening (at sunset) of Friday, until the same time on Saturday; or alternatively, from the evening of Thursday to that of Friday, or from Wednesday to Thursday evening; they will observe the same partial fast as prescribed for the new moon; sunset means [at] the first night star.

In the last two lunations:

The rite is now officiated three times a day; that is also at noon, as well as at sunrise and at sunset.[82]

Both the morning and noon rites will be preceded by ablutions accompanied by the formulas given above, and by a complete and sincere confession of one's sins.

In addition, the negotiation of any business will be abandoned; also strictly avoid the company of anyone except wife, children and closest relatives, and any household servants.

Weekly fasting as in the second two lunations.

One should not enter the oratory without the prescribed sunset rituals, and without burning perfume.

---

82 The circle of the Southern Rite will naturally face south.

Ceremony of Self-Consecration on the Seventh New Moon

On the seventh new moon, the one following the expiration of the sixth moon, the New Moon rite is regularly officiated, having left the shoes outside the oratory.

If the phase falls at night, the dawn of the following day will be awaited for the self-consecration ceremony; also even if it falls after noon, otherwise it will be celebrated following the New Moon Rite.

The window will be open, the oratory lamp (or the two candles) will be lit, the wand and sword ready on the lectern or on the altar, [which is] used for the six-month duration of the preparation.

1) Throw incense on the embers and enter the circle, after marking yourself.

2) Recite the Prayer for the Consecration (given in the *Grimorium*); so:

3) With the right thumb dipped in the previously consecrated holy oil (during the New Moon Rite with the formula given in the *Grimorium* together with its composition), draw the sign of the cross in the middle of your forehead.

If there is an altar, the four corners should also be anointed.

On the four sides of it should also be written with the same oil, and always with the right thumb, verse 24 of Chapter II of Exodus: 'in every place where my name is remembered, I will come and bless you.'

This verse can be transcribed in Latin as well: *In omni loco in quo memoria, fuerit Nominis mei, veniam ad te et benedicam tibi*; as in Hebrew:[83]

בכל המקים אשר אזביר אתי שמי אבאליפ ובר כתיך

The pentacle is also consecrated (figure given in the *Grimorium*), with the formula [which is] given in its place.

Having done this, the consecration having been completed, recite the referral formula given in the *Grimorium*.

After the ordinary daily rite has been officiated, the clothing and the now consecrated magical instruments can be placed; the latter will be placed in a red silk cloth as described in the *Clavicles*,[84] on which the following characters will be written:

---

83 Hebrew is excellent for all as the ritual of Solomonic origin.
84 TN: Mathers 1889, Book Two, Chapter 6-8.

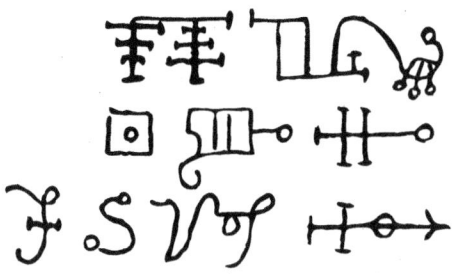

אדני אמתיה אנאירטו
פרימומתון אגלא אין סף
קדוש שמהמפורש[85]

They must never again be taken out of the oratory.

From now on, one will only enter this place with bare feet; and the rites will be officiated with special rope-soled canvas slippers, intended exclusively for the operations of the art.

RULES TO BE OBSERVED AFTER THE CONSECRATION AND FOR THE REST OF ONE'S LIFE

1) After the end of the operation, having also gained power over the elemental spirits [that are] hostile to man, and having come into the possession of the Holy Science, fast for three consecutive days before using it.

Fasts are intended to run from vespers to vespers[86] of the following day, and consists of a single daily meal, not including food from dead animals. It is also allowed to drink water outside of this meal.

2) Every year, the anniversary of the immense grace received from God with the granting of the magical powers will be celebrated.

In particular and by every means, the Guardian Angel will be celebrated and honoured.

3) It is always necessary to continue to officiate the New Moon Rite observing the relative fast, unless contraindicated by the Guardian Angel.

---

85 TN: The Hebrew words are largely divine names from different sources – Adonai, Amathia (from *Goetia*), Anaireton (from *Key of Solomon*), Primeumaton (Hebrew form of the Greek divine name used in the *Key of Solomon* and *Goetia*), Agla, Ain Soph ('Without End' second of the three veils of Negativity beyond the Kabbalistic Tree of Life), Qadosh ('Holy'), Shem HaMephorash (the Ineffable Name of God).

86 TN: Vespers is a service of evening prayer.

4) Parliaments[87] will have to continue, in order to officiate at least one daily rite; the choice of the latter, except for particular instructions from the Guardian Angel, remains at the complete discretion of the operator. The daily invocations to the Planetary Angels of the *Heptamerom*, also present in the *Grimorium* itself, can be adapted to any case; however if the operator prefers a practice that can be traced back more specifically to their own tradition or religion, and can orient it according to the classic ritual instructions belonging to their own faith or philosophy. For example:

a. For Christians, recitation from Psalms 19 and 21 plus verses 1-8 of Psalm 101, followed by a short prayer for the Hermetic Brotherhood.
b. The Jews perform the ordinary recitations of the audience (Shema Israel).[88]
c. The Traditionalists will recite the 'Song of the 22 Runes' and eventual prayer for the Hermetic Brotherhood.
d. The Martinists like Christians in general with prayers for their Order, or Psalms 50 'Miserere mei Domine' and 129 'De Profundis clamavi ad Te Domine'; followed by the same prayer for the Order.
e. The Kremmerzians will officiate the daily Rites of their Brotherhood.[89]
f. Pagans will recite invocations to the planetary Gods, etc.

5) Throughout life one must avoid every vice, every recklessness and every self-indulgence, under pain of falling into power by the spirits that should be dominated.

6) Under no circumstances carry out operations that have not been previously approved, or worse, (those) that have been prohibited by the Guardian Angel.

7) Absolutely avoid confiding to anyone that will be revealed by your Guardian Angel; the only exception is the eventual master who will have initiated us into the practice of this rite.

8) Be absolutely careful not to use this art against your neighbour, except to exercise the penalty eventually commanded by the angels of God.

---

87 TN: The term Parliament here is obviously describing the hierarchy of angels and spirits.

88 TN: The Shema Israel is a primary Jewish prayer, considered to be a daily declaration of faith.

89 TN: The magical system employed by the Corsicans was originated by Giuliano Kremmerz (1861-1930). Kremmerz founded two magical orders, being the Confraternita Terapeutica e Magica di Myriam (The Magical and Therapeutic Brotherhood of Myriam), and the Ordine Osirideo Egiziano (Order of Osiris the Egyptian).

9) Avoid any spirit of revenge and hatred as unseemly to those who serve God, who is of mercy and forgiveness.

10) Beware of practicing any kind of black magic or black sorcery. The only magic allowed, the Divine Royal or Transmutatory Art, also known as alchemy or holy kabbalah, for those who are entitled to it.

11) Never ask your Guardian Angel for any figure or character to operate in evil, although every magician will be requested by countless people. In addition to being useless, such a request would also offend the angel.

12) Before accessing the requests of strangers, whose soul you do not know well, investigate them, inform yourself, in order to avoid that they direct what they have obtained from us to (do) evil things, so that you are not called jointly to pay with them (for) the evil they do.

13) Theoretically, it would be possible to use familiar spirits to harm one's enemies. In practice, however, one should avoid doing true evil; and be content with frightening or warning the insolent and arrogant, so that they can repent; and always only to defend their own inviolable freedom, and for good purposes.

14) When the work of the familiar spirits is sufficient to achieve a certain purpose, avoid employing other spirits.

15) All the more reason to avoid disturbing the four princes of the elements, and the eight vice princes, without a reason of capital importance.

16) Never allow familiar spirits to become too familiar with us. You will never argue with them, also because they usually propose a thousand initiatives together, in order to generate confusion.
The commands will be given to them by voice, instead of through conventional characters and palindromes.

17) Whenever an order is to be given to a spirit other than our Familiars, Psalm 90 is said three times: 'Qui habitat in adjutorio Altissimi'.

18) In working, the spirits will make themselves appear as little as possible, since it must suffice that they respond and obey, and not that they show themselves.

19) All prayers, formulas, operations, conjurations, orders and whatever you want to say, say it loudly and clearly, speaking naturally and pronouncing distinctly, but without shouting and without fidgeting.

20) Apart from cases of absolute urgency, beware of starting any major night operations.

The Great Operation for Contact with the Higher Spirits

After the self-consecration, which will be confirmed by the Guardian Angel according to what will be said below; the operator will first of all seek contact with these and with the higher spirits, if they did not already possess it before; only when they are very well familiar with them, and with the contact technique most suited to them, will they be able to safely carry out the operation to take power over the elementals.

They will therefore begin with the evocation of their own geni, or Guardian Angel to have self-consecration confirmed, and to receive the amount [of contact] necessary to evoke them; and to ask them for assistance of all future operations.

First day

The first evocation of one's Guardian Angel subsequent to self-consecration must always take place in the waning moon of (either) Libra or Aries.

If it does not take place the day after the self-consecration ceremony, it should be done on a Sunday.

If the period of chastity prescribed for the end of the rite of preparation has been interrupted, this evocation must be preceded by at least twenty-two days of abstinence, from each sacrifice to Venus.[90]

Only three days will be enough for the following evocations.

In no case will one work without being in God's grace; that is, stained by serious acts. The day of this evocation having come, get up at sunrise, and without bathing, enter (barefoot) into the oratory; and mark your head with a pinch of ashes taken from the censer or perfume burner, as a sign of humility. You will enter the circle, traced and oriented with all the rules in a solemn form; that is, with the recitation of all the prescribed formulas; therefore, having marked yourself, and holding in the left, or rather hanging from the left forearm, the consecrated sword will be evoked with great intention of one's Guardian Angel through recitation (three or five times):

1) Of the prayer to the Guardian Angel: 'Angel of God who is my guardian, enlighten, guard, rule and govern me ... (name), who was entrusted to you by the Celestial Piety. And so be it.'

The following is then recited:

---

90 TN: I.e. no sex.

2) Great Magical Invocation: 'May the Name always be praised and glorified...' which will be followed by:

3) Invocation: 'Almighty and Everlasting God who created the whole...'
then repeat:

4) Great Invocation; and the Guardian Angel will manifest itself to the sensitive operator.

However, if it still does not appear, repeat the prayer three or five more times: 'Angel of God who is my guardian ...'

If the operator does not perceive the angel by sight, they will nevertheless feel its presence, due to a certain increase in heartbeat, an increase in internal pressure, a feeling of light, or the perception of perfumes, or sounds, or other eloquent phenomena.

However, this means that they do not have the necessary sensitivity to see the angel in human form, and [to] communicate with them.

However, the angel can be summoned for simpler purposes, such as directives of moral conduct, or for other needs. These evocations can also take place before the completion of the preparatory operation; but it would be good for the aspirant to fire magic to familiarize in advance with this practice, which is usually very simple, even just three or five recitations of the angel of God are enough because they manifest at least with the non-visual signs indicated above.

The aspirant who knows his own insufficient sensitivity beforehand will have a sensitive assistant (male or female), who will be available for the day of this first, and subsequent evocations (so that the recitation of the formulas is not disturbed); because at the right moment (sometimes psychics do not last long in magnetic sleep), the operator can put them in an ecstatic condition, so that they can act as an intermediary with the invisible.[91]

---

[91] TN: The sensitive assistant is also known as a 'medium'. Also, see Mathers, 1898, in the Introduction, page xli, entitled Appendix B, 'Employment of A Child Clairvoyant by Cagliostro'.

Characters Useful Both for the Veil of the Sensitive and for that of the Operator

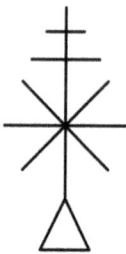

The sensitive can also be asleep with the help of a mirror or a carafe of water.[92]

They will be dressed in white and washed from head to foot. On their head, they will wear a veil of white and transparent silk on which will be written in gold letters (also in gold cut paper), the magic character or the palindrome given below (figure 3).[93]

The operator will also have a veil with the character on his head, but it will be of black silk.

12	13	4	6	148
13	9	148	12	6
4	148	8	148	33
16	23	148	9	15
148	27	4	21	31

U	R	I	E	L
R	I	L	U	E
I	L	I	L	I
E	U	L	I	R
L	E	I	R	U

Palindromes for the Veil of the Sensitive

---

92 On this (matter), see Cahagnet *Magie Magnetique*; Allix *Magnetizer Student's Manual*; L. Petriccione: *Magnetism and Magic*; also Cagliostro *Rituels da la Maconneire Egyptienne*.
TN: *Magie Magnétique ou traité historique et Pratique de Fascinations, Miroirs Cabalistiques, Apports, Suspensions, Talismans, Charme de Vents, Convulsions, Possessions, Envoutements, Sortileges, Magie de la Parole, Correspondance Sympatique, Necromancie, etc* by Louis-Alphonse Cahagnet, Fondateur de la Société des étudiants swedenborgiens, 1858. *Abramelin* mentions this practice of using a sleeping medium/sensitive for the contact.

93 TN: As noted previously, a child is suggested to be used as the medium in *Abramelin*. There are also descriptions of the veils.

A	D	A	M
D	A	R	A
A	R	A	D
M	A	D	A
H	O	M	O

20	1	24	3
1	20	12	24
37	15	20	1
26	40	63	48

Palindromes for the Operator's Veil

When communication with the Guardian Angel has been obtained, in which, to avoid the difficulty of transcribing the characters in magnetic sleep – which not everyone can – you can help yourself, to obtain the figure of the angel, both with a post-hypnotic suggestion: 'The sensitive ... N (name)... as soon as they wake up, they will know him, they will remember it and write it'; both holding a polished silver mirror on the altar, on which the angel will pray to leave the figure. Once the amount has been received, the operator must have the angel confirm the self-consecration.[94]

They will then thank and beg him to take care of them for the rest of his life, and to lead them in the ways of the Lord.

Finally, they will ask him to assist them in the successive evocations of the high spirits, and later also of the elemental and evil spirits, in honour of the Creator, for their own benefit and that of their neighbour.

During these first days, the oratory will no longer be entered.

No one will speak to anyone, nor will anyone be answered, even when it is a question of their wife, children, or servants.

In the evening, after sunset, a sober meal will be allowed.

For all the following seven days, they will sleep alone and observe the most absolute chastity.

Second day

On the second day, according to the same mortification ritual of the previous day, the daily rite is officiated in the morning, at noon, and in the evening, as during the last months of the preparation.

Before going to sleep, the whole body is thoroughly washed with the recitation of the usual formulas.

---

94 However, it should be noted here that it is not always possible to obtain the angel's number in communications.

Third day

On the morning of the third day, the operator will enter (always barefoot) the oratory, having thrown some perfume (incense) on the embers, light the ritual lamp or candles (while) wearing the white linen robe, solemnly trace the circle; and having marked them after entering it, they will thank God for his benefits, and for having been granted the magical powers in particular.

They will then proceed to the evocation of the Guardian Angel with the formulas for the first day (but the recitation of the angel of God should suffice). They will thank him first of all for his help, and his collaboration in the operation; then they will ask him for instructions to evoke other high geni, or at least favorable to man; and to tame the elemental spirits hostile to man (malignant) in due time.

They will be satisfied by the angel after undertaking to obey their suggestions, to strictly follow his instructions, and to no longer voluntarily offend the Creator.

In possession of these instructions, the operator can proceed to the evocation of the high geni, or (those) favorable to man according to the following ritual.

For the Summoning of the High Geni

Upon entering the Magic Circle, recite:

1) The Great Invocation.

2) The conjuration of the angel of the day, with the request of the desired genies: 'Help Me To Summon the Genies...'

3) The Invocation 'Almighty and Everlasting God who created the whole...'

4) Call the desired entity by name; also trace the figure if you have it (if you don't have it, you can always get it through a psychic in a lucid state, if the entity grants it).

5) At the end of the interview, never forget to dismiss the entity with the appropriate formula given in the *Grimorium*.[95]

For the rest of the third day

Throughout this third day, one must remain in communion, that is, in familiar spiritual conversation with one's Guardian Angel, except for an hour of rest granted after noon.

---

95 TN: which is known as the 'License to Depart', in some texts.

During the rest of the day, all the necessary instructions on the elementals, and on how to control them will be received from him; you will take note of these instructions with the utmost care.

At sunset, the usual evening rite is officiated with the ordinary perfume, not forgetting to thank God for the extraordinary grace of the magical powers.

Likewise, we thank the Guardian Angel with a prayer; that he will always continue to assist us.

At the end of the rite, the windows will be left open, and the lamp (or candles) lit, and the door of the oratory closed.

And he may have a frugal dinner before going to rest until the next day.

The evocation of the princes of the elements, the vice princes, and the hostile elementals requires another three days of operation; and can also be done immediately after this one just completed; as for those who do not feel like carrying it out immediately, and would like to postpone it to the next equinox; this would be more than lawful, provided however, that we do not forget to observe in due course, the preventive twenty-two days of chastity prescribed for this evocation, and the one prescribed for the three days it lasts.

THE GREAT OPERATION FOR THE ACQUISITION OF POWER OVER THE PRINCES OF THE ELEMENTS AND THE HOSTILE ELEMENTALS

Provisions common to all three days of the Operation:

The operator gets up before sunrise, lights the lamp (or candles) in the oratory; pours some perfume on the burning embers, and wears the white linen cloth over which he can put the wool robe (or cassock) of any brotherhood to which they belong; if a Christian priest, the golden yellow planet; if Jewish or Muslim, the yellow and gold silk tunic.

For all three days we fast, which is essential to operate; but which will also make us feel freer and more relaxed in body and spirit.

The body and clothes are [kept] clean and neat.

Summoning of the first day

1) Once the circle has been drawn in a solemn form and entered (with the sensitive subject if you do not have the necessary sensitivity to communicate), (with) wand, pentacle and sword at hand (on the lectern), the operator will begin by praying (to) the almighty God, to grant the further grace, to make them happy to complete the Grand Operation (which is) undertaken in praise and glory of His Holy Name, as for his own benefit and for the next.

2) They will also plead with the Guardian Angel to assist them, and to govern their heart and senses in the course of the operation.

3) Then they will hold the wand with their right hand, to pray to God to infuse in it the same virtue, strength and power[96] that he infused in that of Moses, Aaron, Elijah and countless other magicians, but particularly in that of King Solomon.
Then you say:

4) The prayer 'Almighty and everlasting God, in the name of our Lord Jesus Christ', followed by:

5) Psalm 137 and:

6) Conjuration: 'I conjure you, Spirit of the Elements'.

7) Then call the four princes of the elements, which have different names in the various traditions.

We report some of them in order from the succession of the four elements:

	Fuoco (fire)	Aria (air)	Acqua (water)	Terra (earth)
Almadel[97]	Casmaran o Seraf	Talliud o Cherub	Tharsis o Furlac	Ariel o Ardarel
Greek	Antares o Swart	Ondina o Hadchen	Felices o Hodekke	Melide o Hodekket
Arabic	Djin o Sattaaran	Paralda o Rahdar	Nika o Grasgaban	Gobb o Sagladon
	Fuoco	Aria	Acqua	Terra

---

96 TN: From Levi, *The Great Secret Or Occultism Unveiled*, published posthumously in 1898

97 TN: The first line according under the heading Almadel (which refers to the *Ars Almadel* of Solomon), are noted as 'Governing Angels of the Four Seasons' in Barrett, 1801, see Book II, Part III. To note some minor discrepancies, Talliud is considered an angel of water (by Papus in *Traite Elementaire de Science Occulte*, and is also found inscribed on the 7th pantacle of the sun in the Key of Solomon. Seraf is singular for Seraphim, and translates 'fiery serpent'. Additionally, Cherub is singular for Cherubim. Furlac is an angel of earth, according to the Papus text mentioned earlier, and Ardarel is an angel of fire in that same Papus text. Also, the Arabic spirit names here are represented by astrological signs in Levi, 1896:337-338. The Ram - Sattaaran, the Crab - Rahdar, the Balance - Grasgaban, the Goat - Sagladon.

8) When the four princes are called aloud, if they do not present themselves, the prayer is to be recited: 'O Almighty Father, O Wise Son', and repeat:

9) The Conjuration.

If they still do not obey, they are threatened to call the angel St. Michael and all the other angels to force them with their power and their rigor.

Although the Guardian Angel certainly has given the necessary instructions on the subject, we consider it appropriate to remember that this evocation must be carried out with modesty, as a courageous person, but without bravado, without baseness, without too much daring or recklessness.

In case the spirits resist by refusing to obey, do not get angry, as this would seriously harm the irascible operator, and the elemental spirits do not ask for more.

On the contrary, placing all their trust in God, calmly, heartily, the operator will urge them to present themselves by demonstrating that they receive their authority from God, and reminding them of how strong and powerful He is; and also ordering that they show themselves in pleasant and human form.

Having appeared to be the four princes, they will be reminded once again that they are called in the name of the 'Virtue, Power and Authority of the Most High God'.

Then they will be informed not to act under the impulse of malicious curiosity, but in the honour and glory of God; as for their own benefit and that of their neighbour; and therefore the following precepts will be imposed on them:

1) They will be subjected to the operator, as God himself has given power over them.

2) Consequently, whenever they are called, and whatever the service they ask for, they have to appear without delay to obey the orders.

3) In the case of their legitimate impediment, they will send other spirits capable of fulfilling the will of the operator.

They are immediately indicated by name, and swear to obey under penalty of the most rigorous Judgment of God, and punishment by the angels.

Having the four princes agreed to obey, they will designate the eight vice princes and undertake to make them take the oath.

For safety, the wand will be stretched out of the circle, and made to touch each of the four princes while taking the oath.

Then they are sent back by telling them to go back to their usual locations, and (to be) ready to show up whenever they are called.

Evocation of the second day

Having officiated the ordinary daily rite in the morning, observing all the ritual details (circle in solemn form), the four princes will be invoked briefly by reciting the following:

1) Conjuration. They will appear immediately, (then) remind them of the promises and the oath taken the day before; they will be invited to present the eight vice princes. For this purpose it is recited:

2) The prayer: 'Oh Father Almighty, Oh Wise Son', followed by the preceding one:

3) Conjuration, both as addressed to all twelve princes and vice princes.

It appears that they are also the latter, they will be made to swear after giving the same warnings made to the four princes the day before.

From each of these, the operator will be assigned a familiar spirit, what they have the duty to do

Shifts, duties and other details of these spirits are given below, before the instructions to be given on the third day.

Both the eight vice princes and the four familiar spirits, after they have sworn, will be given the summoning numbers; and then all take their leave, (while) ordering them to appear the next morning.

The formula for the ordinary reference is inserted in the *Grimorium*, and will be used in all subsequent evocations. The elementals obey it very readily, as they do not like being in the presence of the magician.

Before dismissing them, the four familiar spirits will be ordered to regularly present themselves to their shifts which are - Fire, hour 6-12; Air, hour 12-18; Water, hour 18-24; Earth, hour 0-6; (while) remaining in the form commanded by the operator for all six of their hours.

Evocation of the third day

The prayers and conjurations on the third day are the same as on the second day, but are now intended to have the eight vice princes present with all their subordinates, to be reminded of their promises and oaths from the previous day.

This done, the vice prince of the element fire will be ordered to visibly appear, with all his subordinates in the form that the angel will indicate.

The same warnings (are) made to the princes and vice princes, and similar requirements; therefore they will be sworn to appear whenever they are called by name.

They will then jointly call themselves the (first degree) vice prince of the element fire and the (first degree) of the element earth; and will be sworn in obedience together with their common subordinates.

The same will be done in conjunction with the (first degree) vice prince of the element earth and the (first degree) of the element water with their common subordinates.

Then they will call together the (first degree) vice prince of the element water, and of the element air, and we will do the same.

The same thing will be done with the second vice princes, two by two with the common subordinates.

Reference in the usual form.

How to Deal with the Elemental Spirits and Resist their Subtle Demands

Both the princes of the elements and all the other elementals always try, and in every way to resist the power of the new magician; to set traps for him, to be compensated in some way for the services rendered to them; to establish the principle of the 'pact'; to borrow directly or indirectly, (through) sacrifice or adoration.

First of all, the four princes will try to put him in difficulty by asking him 'Who is He who has given him so much authority'.

They will reproach him for his daring and his presumption to call them, as he is so weak and sinful.

They will blame him for his sins, and try to question his science, his religiosity, his morality and his faith in God.

For example, to the Christian they will say: 'What do you have to do with these Solomonic Rites, when you are steeped in polytheism and idolatry?' To the polytheist they will say: 'What do you and the other creatures of your faith have to do with the One God of Israel, if you don't even know him?'[98]

They will tell the Israelite that his faith and his religion have now been rejected by God, and that he does not observe the new law.

He should answer calmly and in a nutshell:

1) That these dealings do not concern them.

2) You are not called to express your opinion on the matter.

3) That, however great sinners we are, we hope that the true and only God, who created heaven and earth, and who subjected them to us, and obliged them to obey us, will have forgiven us our sins; and that for the future, what that will be our religion, we will only come to recognize, confess and honor others but Him.

---

98 TN: See Mathers, 1898, Book II, chapter XVII.

The elementals and their princes know well that the power of the new magician is legitimate and regular, and that therefore they are obliged to obey him, without asking him for anything in return; however they always seek to obtain payment of the requested services, even insignificant objects, such as a hair of his head, or a hair of an animal, to implicitly affirm the prince that the magician does not actually or fully possess his power, and therefore (they) attempt to bargain with him.

These agreements are to be avoided and rejected absolutely, because the requests would get worse and worse in the future. Considering that there is no need to concede anything, and that the most insignificant requests conceal something else, one must not give in to anything.

The angel will certainly have given instructions on the subject: 'If the spirit asks for something, refuse firmly without deflecting, but also without exaggerating in severity'.

Of the offers to obey after having stipulated special covenants or conditions, one replies: 'God our Lord has condemned you to obey me, and to serve me without covenants or conditions, and I cannot grant them'.

They will also ask for some sacrifices, even in the form of special courtesies; if one wishes to be served and obeyed promptly; it will be answered that the sacrifices are not made to them, but only to God.

Then, they will cease not to repress or oppose the black magicians and sorcerers under them, and not to use holy wisdom against them.

It will be answered that, we are obliged to pursue the enemies of God, to suppress their malice, to save and defend our neighbours, and the people offended and damaged by the spirits hostile to man, and by the evil sorcerers subject to them.

The elementals usually besiege the new magician with great verbal assaults; sometimes they even engage in collective rioting or showing unspeakable anger.

The magician does not show anger with fear, instead (they) do not appear concerned, and show them the consecrated magic wand.

If they continue to tumult, just strike the wand two or three times on the lectern, or on the altar if you have one, and immediately the quiet will return.

The familiar spirits in turn usually ask the magician to promise not to give them to anyone.

Stand firm and do not promise anything to anyone, replying that everyone is obliged to help friends with all their means and possibilities, including the use of some familiar spirit.

If a spirit is proud, treat him this way; if, however, he is humble, do not show yourselves (to be) too rude or too severe, practicing moderation in everything.

When finally the spirits have lost all hope of overcoming the operator, and they will have realised that they can not get anything; (then) they will give up, and will only beg him not to be too rude, and demanding in ordering them.

We will then answer that if they are ready to obey, we can get the angel to advise us not to be too rigid.

In speaking to the spirits, in any case avoid using words that are not well understood or the meaning is not fully known, under pain of great shame and harm.

In essence, the magician must behave with the spirits as their lord, and not as their servant.[99]

And as a gentleman he must know well what he can expect of them, and what is not allowed.

Faced with the refusal of a spirit, first make sure that what is asked of it falls within its possibilities, since each spirit has its own skills – sometimes admirable and prodigious, but still limited to its own area of expertise - and is neither omniscient nor omnipotent.

So beware of pretending to force him to obey before you are certain of his specific abilities.

In the house of disobedience or rejection on the part of a spirit, his superiors will be called; and they will be reminded of the oaths they have taken, and of the punishments that await the violators.

Faced with a firm attitude, every spirit will obey, but in case of persistence of the refusal, call the Guardian Angel who will punish.

However, always avoid using rigor, when it can be achieved with the right firmness.

After the postponement of the elementals and their princes, never forget to purify the place with incense.

The Nine Rules of Transmitting the Rite to Others

1) The rite to attain the powers of fire magic is legitimately transmitted from father to son (only one) for three generations, and no more.

In addition to this hereditary transmission, it can be transmitted by each magician to no more than two disciples.

2) In the case of transmission also to a third person, it will work for this, but the magician who has granted it will lose all power.

3) Before granting this rite to a monarch, inquire above if the candidate is worthy; and if he will be worthy in the future, since whoever grants it, responds jointly with the one who receives it, of the evil that the latter could do.

And a head of state, of evil even if only by mistake, can do a lot.

---

99 TN: See Mathers, 1898, Book II, chapter XVIII.

4) The rite will never be given to a non-monarchical head of state, nor to any person involved in politics.

The state regiments other than the holy monarchy, founded on the royal art, are nothing more than criminal associations, intended to have the majority of the population oppressed by another part of it; and therefore the magical power in the hands of such politicians, and be certain that it would serve no other purpose than crime, like all other means at their disposal.

The granting magician would thus become their accomplice, and would be called to respond with them.

5) The rite can only be transmitted free of charge and never sold; whoever sells it will lose all power, and suffer severe punishment.

6) It is prescribed that whoever grants the rite requires sworn promise from whoever receives it, never to transmit it for remuneration, nor to grant it to any of the persons indicated above, nor to impious or atheist persons.

7) Although the soul of men cannot be fully known except by God, before introducing someone into this branch of magic, it is necessary to probe their soul in every way.

His life and customs will be examined; we will discuss the matter with him without opinion, trying to understand if such a person will use the magical power for good or for evil.

8) In giving the rite to someone, (they will) fast by eating only once a day, as for the lunar fast.

Those who receive it will follow the same norm.

Everyone is careful not to fail in this, as it is an essential condition for the effectiveness of the transmission.

9) Finally, anyone who has received the rite will be given any favour that is not in terms of money, to be carried out through the power achieved.

END OF INSTRUCTIONS

PRAISE GOD (LAUS DEO)

The Familiar Spirits

The first four vice princes of the elementals assign the familiar spirits, one for each of them.

In reality, each man can manage to have up to four familiar or household spirits (in the sense of servants: famuli or familiars) and no more; these spirits can offer their services in many fields.

The first of the four spirits carries out its functions from sunrise to noon; the second from noon to sunset; the third from sunset to midnight, and the fourth from midnight to sunrise the following day.

Those who possess them are free to let them take the form (that) they like best.

There is an infinite number of these spirits, who from the time of their fall were condemned to serve men; each man having four, and are obliged to a daily service of six hours each.

If you give one to someone, you won't be able to use it anymore, but you can replace it with another spirit.

If you want to dismiss the spirit before the six hours of his shift, just signal him to leave; otherwise, as soon as his hours of service have elapsed, the spirit will go away spontaneously, without asking permission, while the next one arrives.

Familiar spirits are very ready and serve perfectly in the tasks in which it is appropriate to occupy them, such as in painting, in history, for making watches, sculpting or shaping statues, making weapons, or other similar tasks.[100]

They are employed in chemistry, they are made to carry out trade in the form of other people, they are made to transport merchandise or other effects, they are used to quell disputes and fights, to prevent murders, and all kinds of evils and of malefics, to carry letters to all countries, to free prisoners, and a thousand other offices that can be learned from experience.

When you ask each of the competent sub-princes for your familiar spirits, you will have their names told you, which you will write down immediately, with an indication of the time for which they are obliged to serve you.

Then submit the palindromes to your familiar spirits[101] concerning the forms you want them to take. You will make them swear, not only collectively, but separately, that from that moment on they will duly observe the six hours of service for you; and you will be promised that they will do everything you command them with loyalty without deceit or lies.

And if by chance you give any of them to another person, they will have to be faithful as you are.

---

100 TN: See Mathers, 1898, Second Book, 20th chapter.

101 Excellent palindromes contained in the *Arsenal Manuscript* published under the title *La Magie Sacree* (Paris), translated and published in the third volume of *Secret Magic*, by Edizioni Rebis.
TN: These are presented in, Mathers 1898: 163-247.

Finally, that they have to fulfill and execute what God has inflicted on them, as a punishment with a just and irrevocable sentence.

May the magician practice it with royal wisdom, since the divine law exists above the laws of man; and glory be eternally rendered to the supreme Lord in the high heaven.

Appendix: Of the Skills of Evil or Elemental Spirits

The elemental or evil spirits are very numerous; we will limit ourselves here to giving the names of the four princes or higher spirits, and of the eight ministers or vice-princes, according to *Abramelin*.[102]

The four princes are:

LUCIFER
LEVIATHAN
SATAN
BELIAL

The eight vice-princes are:

ASTAROT
MAGOT
ASMODEO
BELZEBU
ORIENS
PAIMONE
ARITON
AMAYMONE

In some rituals, the last four are given different names; they follow the princes and vice-princes according to the season and the element.[103]

---

102 TN: Mathers, 1898:104-122.

103 TN: There are a few minor spelling discrepancies in Abramelin, ie: Asmodee, Belzebud and Amaimon.

Fire	East	Spring	(Salamanders): Lucifer, Astarot and Oriens
Air	South	Summer	(Sylphs): Belial, Belzebu and Amaymone
Water	West	Autumn	(Ondine): Leviathan, Magot and Paimone
Earth	North	Winter	(Gnomes): Satan, Asmodeus, Ariton and Egino[104]

Always in the same order we report some names, in different traditions, of the princes of the elements:

Seraf	Casmaran	Antares	Djin	Sattaaran	Malchidael	
Cherub	Talliud	Ondina	Hadchen	Parala	Radar	Muriel
Tharsis	Furlac	Felices	Hoddeken	Nika	Grasgarban	Casadel
Ariel	Ardael	Melide	Odekket	Gobb	Sagdalon	Beriel

Second: ALMADEL = GREEK = ARAB = HEBREW

The particular conjurations for each of the twelve spirits are found in Eliphas Levi (*Ritual*) and in Pope Honorius's Grimoire.[105]

Let's see their specific skills here:[106]

ASTAROT and ASMODEO together carry out the mining works: quarrying, mining and extractive works in general.

Chemical work and operation on metals; teaching chemistry; transformation of animals into men and of men into animals.

ASMODEO and MAGOT together carry out the work of bringing food and drinks to the operator, in unlimited quantities.

ASTAROT and ARITON – EGINO – GOBB they seek and allow to acquire treasures, whatever they are, as long as they are not seen, using their ministers, but they do not work in collaboration, but rather separately.

---

104 TN: See Mathers, 1898, Second Book, 15th Chapter, in footnote, it is stated: 'Ariton is often called Egin or Egyn in other works on magic.'

105 Reported in the first volume of *Secret Magic*, Edizioni Rebis.
TN: Also, see Rankine & Barron, 2013. I assume the editor is referring to the Prayers of the Salamanders, Sylphs, Ondines and Gnomes, as presented in Appendix A.

106 TN: Also, see, Mathers 1898:138-149.

ORIENTE – PAYMONE – ARITON – AMAYMONE,[107] or also:

MAYMONE – PAYMONE – EGINO – AMAYMONE carry out through their common ministers, the operations to know anything of the past and the future; they give information and clarifications on every kind of controversial science; they make any spirit appear in the desired form; they give visions in mirrors, crystals and other means.

They provide the familiar spirits; they animate dead bodies, and make them act as if they are alive for seven years.

They allow the operator to fly in the air and go anywhere by splitting up; they make the desired visions appear; they make armed armies appear.

AMAIMONE and ARITON – EGINO together operate the opening and closing of all kinds of locks, without keys and without noise.

ORIENTE-MAYMONE alone provide as much money as you want to provide for your needs, and live in opulence.

PAYMONE brings up armed armies.

ARITON-EGINO discovers the thefts carried out.

AMAYMONE heals diseases and wounds.

ASTAROT excites storms and demolishes buildings and fortifications.

MAGOT prevents and annuls all operations of necromancy and low magic; destroying its effects, except the operations of kabbalah and divine magic; he recovers all kinds of lost or stolen books. Makes the operator assume the shape or figure requested by him.

Discovers thefts; has all sorts of musical, theatrical shows, etc ... represented at the request of the operator.

ASMODEO reveals people's secrets to the operator, however jealously guarded.

BELZEBU transforms animals into men and vice versa; he excites all sorts of hatred, enmity, discord, quarrels, disputes, fights, battles and pains.

---

107 TN: It is noted repeatedly in Mathers, 1898, third book, 'Oriens, Paymon, Ariton, and Amaymon execute the operations hereof by means of their common ministers.'

Also very important and fundamental are the competences and attributions of the familiar spirits which, as mentioned above, are granted by the four vice-princes ORIENTE, PAYMONE, ARITON, AMAYMONE.

Familiar spirits provide information and clarification in all sorts of controversial sciences; they give visions in mirrors and other means; they reveal the secrets of the people to the operator who requests them, however jealously guarded they are; they intervene for affection and love matters.

They heal diseases, demolish buildings and castles; discover thefts, bring out the desired visions, provide the money necessary to provide for their own needs, and live in opulence.

They have plays of all kinds of shows.

FINISH

Premise

The *Book of Shadows* (*Liber Umbrarum*) is an authentically magical, very mysterious text.

Dictated to a disciple by a master of a Rosicrucian magical school in 1573, who in turn had received it from unknown masters; and it has come down to us intact through time, transcribed by hands tied to invisible chains.[108]

Precious active and pulsating instrument of the arcane arts, the qualitative level clearly superior to the other texts of a similar subject appears immediately evident in the eyes of the expert scholar of ancient magic, thus assuming an extremely symbolic character as well as eminently operational.

It is mostly spoken of in the most authoritative treatises on magic and occultism, but never in the world had the divine grimoire appeared in its integral guise and in all its power. Therefore, those who intend to apply the powers that the volume conceals should know how the guardian of the threshold watches attentively and relentlessly, against the profaners of the sacred temple.

Istibus[109]

---

108 TN: Levi, 1973:161, from the appendix entitled 'Doctrine of Eliphas Levi' by Papus (Gerard Encausse): '... thus they form great invisible chains and can occassion or determine vast elemental upheavals.'

109 TN: Istibus is a pseudonym for Luca Pierini.

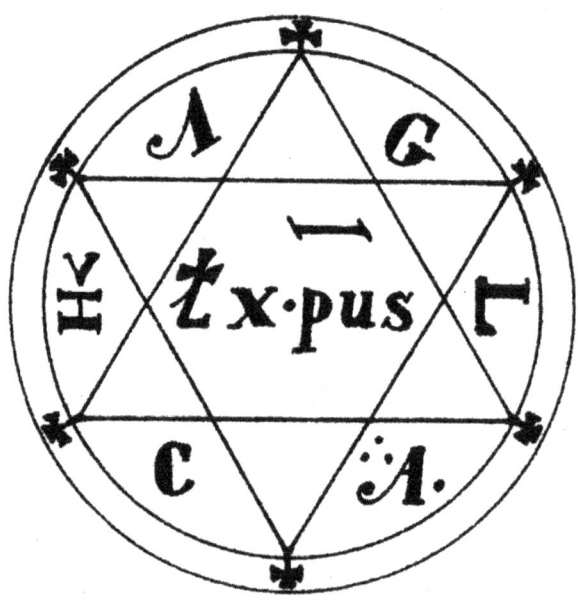

To the Knights of the Holy Kingdom

You know, wise philosophers of the qabalistic art, that in this work, I have enclosed the most precious treasure of the universe, and the most important secrets of the supreme magic dictated by the angel Metatron. I give these pages of golden wisdom to you, worthy heirs of the art of kings, and I await your work. Be faithful to the divine laws of nature, since only from the seed of goodness can the smell of goodness be born fruitful, of nourishment for the roots of the sacred tree. This great magic book hides the first secret key of the invisible world; the sages comprehend of the arcanum... I pray with sincere heart to the less wise, and await the divine sign of the ancient celestial masters – may the angel of the Lord illuminate our path in the kingdom of the magus; that the sun, the moon and the stars be our guide in the celestial gardens of art; and let the sacred flame of the divine fire that burns secretly in the hearts of the philosophers of the great work shine forever.
Amen.

Formula of Exorcism

'I exorcise you, O Book, for Truth, Life, Eternity, and I purify you from any extraneous influence or contamination.'

Conjuring Formula

'I conjure you O book, that you are profitable in making use of you legitimately, in any operation. ✠ I adjure you by the virtue of the saint's name Agla ✠ On ✠ Tetragrammaton ✠ that you are useful to those who will read you with divine grace in the heart.'[110]

Formula of Consecration

'O Adonay Ieve[111] Tzebaot, O Supreme Father, Creator of heaven and earth, of the three, of the four, and of the seven. The ineffable one, I beseech you, by your powers and your virtues, to accept the sacrament of this book that I make to you, having prepared it in your honour – Enjoy sanctifying it.'[112]

The Sword

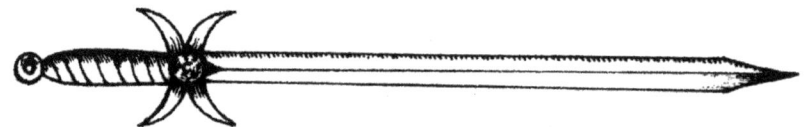

THE ART OF COMMANDING SPIRITS OF THE HOLY KINGDOM
Seven Year Daily Ritual to Attain the Practice of the Magic of Fire

This ceremony, which precedes the life of the great operation, serves to obtain in the operator, the necessary dignity to operate in the invisible world. The ceremony must be officiated in the magic circle every day, before or after the sunrise; giving the particular conjuration to the archangel who dominates the day: Sunday to Michael, Monday to Gabriel, and so on. It started with the new moon of

---

110 TN: Also, see 'Conjuration of the Book' in Rankine & Barron, 2013:112-113.
111 TN: Ieve is Yod Heh Vau Heh, the Tetragrammaton.
112 TN: See Mathers, 1889, Book Two, chapter XXII, 'Consecration of the Book'.

Aries, or even in another moon, even starting on a Sunday. For the entire duration of the course, the beginning of pure life is to be observed, charity is practiced, food is provided, with the exclusion of foods from dead animals. Wash completely on Monday and Friday. Wash the room of the operation frequently with running water; no one enters it other than the operator himself. By carefully observing this purifying practice, the first contacts with the higher spirits can be obtained. After this, contact with other genies will be lost; and finally, it will be possible to attempt evocation, and domination over the elemental and evil spirits.

The Figure of the Cabalistic Magic Circle of Solomon[113]

---

113 TN: Talismanic diagram with Hebrew lettering and Latin: *Deus Vivus - Deus Verus - Deus Sanctus* ('The Living God - The Real God - The Holy God'). In the centre of the triangle: Yod / Yod Heh / Yod Heh Vau / Yod Heh Vau Heh. Hebrew in outer circle: IH; ALHI ISATh ✠ IHO; ALHI ABRHAM ✠ (ISATH is possibly Isaac, in which case the translation would read 'The Lord God of Isaac, Lord God of Abraham'). The triangle in centre including Yod Heh Vau Heh matches up with the Talisman for the Invocation for Thursday (Jupiter), on page 16 of *Secret Grimoire of Turiel*, (attributed to) Marius Malchus, Aquarian Press, 1960. This was said to be discovered in 1927, written in Latin and dating to 1518, although it is unlikely and considered to be quite spurious. It is however most certainly derived from the *Arbatel of Magick, Concerning The Magic of the Ancients* (translated to English by Robert Turner, London, 1655) which was included in *Fourth Book of Occult Philosophy*.

Of the Way to Make the Circle

The circle is drawn with charcoal or chalk, or even with the thumb of the right hand used as a rod. First, they will have sprinkled the water and salt around, saying:

Aelohi Abraham ✠ Aelohi Isaac ✠ Aelohi Jacob! +[114]

The book is consecrated by placing it in a triangle outside the circle, and making them look on it faithfully by each spirit, in the name of the Most High God Tetragrammaton, placing their open hand on it.

What is to be Said While Making the Magic Circle[115]

Lord, we have heard from your virtue. Lord, confirm this work. May what is done by us (here) be as the cornerstone of the temple, and the angel of the Lord comes to serve us for Alpha and Omega, Eloy, Elohim, Elohe, Zebaoth, Elion, Hezekiah, Adonay, Jah, Tetragrammaton, and Shadday.

The earth and all those who live there belong to the most high God, because he founded it on the sea, and prepared it on the rivers. Who is the one who goes up the mountain of the Lord? And who is the one who will be sent to the Holy Place? The innocent of hand and pure of heart, who has not conquered his soul in vain; who has not sworn falsely to his neighbour; he will be blessed by God and he will receive mercy for his health.

Princes, open your doors. Open the eternal doors, and the king of glory will enter. Who is this king of glory? The omnipotent Lord, the Lord and the king of glory.

Enter only he who walks on asp and basilisk, and who has reconciled the lion and the dragon: He who opened the Book of Seven Seals.

But no adverse power will enter, since:

Qui habitat in adjutorio Altissimi, in protectione Dei coeli commorabitur.

---

114 TN: Aelohi is spelled out in the manuscript, which probably means 'Elohi', so the prayer is 'God of Abraham, God of Isaac, God of Jacob'.
115 TN: See, Mathers, 1889, Book One, Chapter III, for a detailed description of the construction of the circle.

Salvum fac servum tuume.
Deus meus, sperantem in te.
Esto ei Domine turris fortitudinis
a facie inimici.
Nihil proficiat inimicus in eo.
Et filius iniquitatis non apponat vocere ei.
Mitte ei Domine auxilium de Sancto.
Et de Sion tuere eum.
Domine, exaudi orationem ueam.
Et clamor meus ad te veniat.

Operatore: Dominus vobiscum.
Assistenti: Et cum Spiritu Tuo.

(Translation)

'He who dwells in the aid of the Most High will abide under the protection of God of heaven. Save your servant. My God who trusts in you. Be unto him, Lord, tower of strength before the face of the enemy. Let the enemy gain nothing from him. And let not the son of iniquity set his voice before him. Send him help, Lord, from the Holy One. And protect him from Zion. Lord, hear my prayer. And let my cry come to you.'

Operator: 'The Lord be with you.'
Assistant: 'And with your Spirit.'

EXECUTION

Draw the circle, oriented in the direction prescribed for the day; enter and draw the word IEVE[116] in Hebrew characters in the centre from right to left, as shown in the figure.

The operator, equipped with a censer and taking ash from the incense burner, will mark himself with the secret cabbalistic cross:

Tibi sunt ✠ Malcuth ✠ Geborah ✠ Scesed ✠ Per Aeonas.[117]

---

116 TN: Yod Heh Vau Heh.
117 TN: You are ✠ the kingdom (Malkuth) ✠ the strength (Geburah) ✠ the mercy (Chesed) ✠ through the ages. See Levi 1896:234, describing this prayer as the occult version of the Lord's Prayer. As David Rankine observed in private correspondence, this is clearly the origin of the Qabalistic Cross in the Lesser Banishing Ritual of the Pentagram created by the Hermetic Order of the Golden Dawn.

Then, with the right hand raised up, the palm open, the fingers outstretched, speak the following prayer:

Dixitque Manoach as Angelum Domini: Obsecro te ut acquiescas precibus meis, et faciamus tibi haedum de capris. Cui respondit angelus: Si ne cogis, uon comedam panes tuos: si autem vis holoraustum facere, offer illud Domino. Et nesciebat Manoach quod angelus Domini esset. Dixitque ad cum: Quod est tibi nomen, ut, si sermo tuus fuerit expletus, honoremus te? Cui ille respondit: Cur quaeris nomen meum, quod est mirabile? Julit itaque Manoach haedum de capris et libamenta, et posuit super petram, offerens Domino qui facit mirabilia; ipse autem et uxor ejus intuebantur. Cum ascenderet flamma altaris in aelum. Angelus Domini pariter in flamma ascendit. Quod cum vidissent Manoach et uxor efus, proni caeciderunt, in terram, et ultra eis non apparuit angelus Domini. Statimque intellexit Manoach angelum Domini esse, et dixit ad uxorem suam: Morte moeriemur, quia uidimus Deum. Cui respondit mulier: Si Dominus non vellet occidere, de manibus nostris holocaustum et libamenta non suscepisset, nec ostendisset nobis haec omnia, neque ea quae sunt ventura dixisset.

(Translation)

And Manoach said as the angel of the Lord: Please consent to my request, and let us prepare for you a kid. And the angel answered him: If thou forces me, I will not eat thy bread: but if thou wilt make a burnt offering, offer it to the Lord. And Manoach did not know that it was the angel of the Lord. And he said to him: What is your name, that, if your word be accomplished, we may honor you? And he answered him: Why do you ask my name, which is amazing? And show Manoach the kid, and the libations, and put it on a rock, offering it to the Lord, who does wonders; he and his wife looked on when the flame from the altar ascended to heaven. The angel of the Lord ascends in the same flame. When Manoach and his wife saw this, they fell to the ground, on their face and the angel of the Lord appeared to them no more. And immediately Manoach understood that it was the angel of the Lord, and said to his wife: We shall surely die, because we have seen God. And the woman answered him: If the Lord would not kill, he would not have received from our hands the holocaust and the libations, nor had he known to us all these things, nor had said the things that are to come.

At this point, the incense is placed on the embers of the perfume burner or the censer, and the following is the beginning:

Prayer of Request

Omnipotens sempiterne Deus, qui dignatus es uniterre angelos tuos servis servabusque tuis: Abraham, Agar, Moises, Manoach, Elias, Gad, Josues, Jacob, Gedeoni, Loth, Israeli, Davidi, Josef, Zacharie, Danieli, Marie Madalenae, et aliis innumeribus, qui per eos, illos protexisti, instruxisti et duxisti ad portum novissimum salutis, et introduxisti in aeterna gaudia, supplex te rogo, ut peccata mea remittas, et misericordia ac benevolentia recipias orationem hanc, qua te fatigo ad obtinendum, ex misericordia tua, comitatus sanctorum angelorum tuorum. Haec peto, Domine, Deus pietatis, Deus Patiens, Benignissime, Liberalissime, Saggissime qui gratias tuas non uno inodo accordas, qui obliviscceris iniquitates, peccata et flagitia hominum, in cospectu ufus, nemo innoxius probatus est, qui visitas culpas, patrum in filiis et in nepotibus, usque ad quarta generationem, quia conosco miseriam meam, nec dignus sum apparere ante divinam majiestatem tuam, nec implorare et horare clementiam tuam, tuamque misericordiam pro minima gratia. Sed tamen, Domine dominorum, tuam magna est fons bonitatum tuarum, ut illa ipse appellet quos pudent peccatorum suorum, et eos invitet ad recipiendas gratias suas. Te supplicor igitur, Domine Deus meus, ut miserearis mei et omnem malitiam ac iniquitatem meam tollas. Munda animam meam de omne foeditate peccati, spiritum meum redintegra in me, et in cum reconforta ut fortis sit ac misterium tuae gratiae et thesaura tuae sapientiae intelligere possit. Cum oleo sanctificationis tuae sanctifica me sicut omnes servos tuos, propretas sanctificasti. Per hunc oleum, omnia quae mihi sunt, sanctifica in me, ut dignus factus sim de Sanctis Angelis Tuis, ut cum eis agere possim, et de eis et per eos notitias, recipere, et dominium in Divinam Sapientiam Tuam. Omni potens sempiterne Deus, qui creationem totam ad gloriam et honorem tuum fecisti, nec non ad utilitatem hominis, supplex te rogo, ut Genium vel Genios meos, ordinis solaris, as me mittere digneris ad instaurandam communicationem et commercium inter nos; ut ego ...N... possim eos cognoscere et cognitiones recipere ab eis me doceant de omnibus quibus eos interrogaverno, vel ut remedia omnia a me quaesita, contra hydropissiam; cancerum, vel alium quemquam malum, me donent. Et hoc fiat non ex mea, sed tus voluntate, in nomine Jesu Christi, filii tui unici, Domini nostri. Amen. Omnipotens Sempiterne Deus, Domine Coeli et Terra, Formator et Creator omnium visibilium et invisibilium, Ego ...N... Servus Tuus indignus, Te invoco secundum ipsum jussum Tuum, per nomen Filii Tui Unici Jesu Christi Domini Nostri et per arcanam virtutem sanctissimi Nominis Ejus:

יהשוה (Jehosciua)[118]

Ut ad ne mittere digneris Spiritum Sanctum Tuum qui ne dirigat in tus veritate ad absolutum bonum Tuum. Non ardentissime appeto dominium in Scientiam Vitae, cum cognitione perfecta de ubus mihi necessariis, Scientia obscurissimam quam, sine auxilio Tuo penetrare non potere: concede mihi quisque de Angelis, Geniis vel Spiritibus Tuis, qui me doceat regulas illas Sanctae Sapientiae, quae nobis discendae sunt ex ipso voluntate Tua in Te Caudando et honorando, atque ad adjurandum proximum nostrum da mi hi docilitatem cordis ut faciliter discam omnia que doceas me, et ea in animo meo recipiam, ad ipsa expandenda sicut rivus inexauribilium thesaurorum Tuorum, pro omnibus causis justis, et etiam concede mihi gratiam hanc, ut de his excelsis beneficiis in humile timore et timida reverentia utar.

Omnipotens sempiterne Deus, in nomine Domini Nostri Jesu Christi, Patriis et Filii et Spiritus Sancti, Sancta Trinitas et inseparabilis Unitas, te invoco ut sis mihi salus et defensio, et pratectio corporis et animae meae et omnium verum mearum. Per virtutem ✠ Sanctae Crucis, et per Virtutem Passionis Tuae, deprecor te, Domine Jesu Christi, per merita Beatissimae Mariae Virginis et matris tuae, atque omnium sanctorum tuorum, ut mihi concedas gratiam et potestatem divinam in omnes sanctos Angelos tuos, atque in spiritus elementorum et etiam in malignos spiritus, ut secundum statum, conditionem et potestatem eorum, quoscumque nominibus invocavero vel evocavero statim ex omni parte conveniant, et voluntatem meam perfecte adimpleant, quod maligni, mihi nihil nocentes, neque timorem inferentes, sed potens obedientes et ministrantes, tua distincto virtute percipiente, mandata mea perficiant. Amen.

Cadosh, Cadosh, Cadosh, Dominus Deus Sabaoth, qui venturus es judicare vivos et mortuos: Ju qui es Primus et Novissimus, Rex Regum et Dominus Dominantium, El ✠ Elohim ✠ Elche ✠ Zebaoth ✠ Elion ✠ Ascierceie ✠ Adonay ✠ Jah ✠ Tetragrammaton ✠ Shadday ✠ Ischiros ✠ Aghios ✠ Eleison Jmas ✠ Agla ✠ Messias ✠; per haec tua sancta nomina et per haec alia: Iod ✠ Ieus ✠ Elchim ✠ Chibor ✠ Eloha ✠ Elohim Zebaoth ✠ Ieve Zebaoth ✠ Elhay ✠ Adonay Melech ✠ et per omnia alia Tua nomina, Je invoco et obsecro, Domine Jesu Christe, per Nativitatem et Baptismum Tuum, per Passionem et Crucem Tuam, per Ascensionem Tuam, per Adventum Spiritus Sancti Paracliti , per amaritudinem animae Tuae quondo e✠ivit de corpore tuo per quinque vulnera tua, per sanguinem et per aquam qui e✠ierant de corpore tuo, per Virtutem

---

118 TN: From the context this is clearly Yeheshuah – Yod Heh Shin Vau Heh (in the original the fourth letter is a badly drawn Vau), the Pentagrammaton which is Jesus. The word Jehosciua is probably a miscopying or strange version of Jeheshuah.

Tuam, per sacramentum quod dediste Discipulis Tuis pridie passionis tuae, per Sanctam Trinitatem, per Individuam Unitate, per Beatam Mariae matron Tuam, per Angelos et Archangelos, et Prophetas et Patriarchas, et per omnes Sanctos Tuos, et per omnia Sacramenta quae fiant in honore Tuo, adoro et je, obsecro je, Benedico Tibi, et rogo ut acceptes oratione has et summam potentiam dones his conjurationibus et verbis omnibus oris mei, quibus, uti voluero, per Dominum Jesum Christum, Deus nostrae salutis: da mihi virtutem et potestatem tuam super omnes angelos tuos, sive in Coelo stantes, sive de Coelo efecti ad decipiendum humanum genus, et super spiritus elementorum, sive ignis, et aeris, et aquae aut ignis, ad attra handum eos, ad costringendum, ad legandum eos pariter et solvendum; et ad congregandum eos coram me, ut quae possunt, faciant et verba mea, vocemque meam nullo modo contemnant, sed mihi et dictis meis obcediant, et me timeant. Per humanitatem et misericordiam et gratiam Tuam deprecor et peto ✠ per Potentiam et Virtutem Dei Patris ✠ per sapientiam Filii Redentoris omnium hominum et per ✠ Clementiam spiritus Sancti: id est ✠ per Quem Legem titam complevit ✠ Qui est ✠ erat ✠ et semper erit ✠ Omnipotems ✠ Aghios ✠ Iskyros ✠ Athanatos ✠ Soter ✠ Tetragrammaton ✠ Jeova ✠ Alpha et Omega, et per omnia Tua Sancta, et per omnes Sanctos et Sanctas Tuas, per Angelos et Archangelos, Potestates, Dominationes et Virtutes, et per illum Nomen per quod Salomo constringebat daemonem et oboediebatur ab ipso. Et per El, Elohim, Elohe, Zebaoth, Elion, Eieie ascer eieie, Adonay, Jah, Tetragrammaton, Shadday, et per omnia tua nomina quae scripta sunt in hoc libro, et per virtutem corumdem, quaetenus me potens facias congregare, constringere, omnes tuos spiritus, sive in Coelo stantes, sive de Coelo repulsos, sive spiritus elementorum sint, ut mihi veraciter de omnibus meis quaestionibus interrogatis, de quibus quaeram, veracem responsum tribuant, et omnibus meis mandatis satifasciant, sine laesione corporis et animae meae et omnium ad me pertinentuim. Da mihi Domine, potestatem quam concessiste servis tuis et Prophetis in omnes Spiritus, sive Angelos, sive Spiritus Elementorum uti Salomandras, Pygmaeos, Fatas, Driades, Sylvanos, Nymphas, Gnomos, Ondinas et Sylphos. O Pater Omnipotens, O Filii Sapiens, O Spiritus Sancte corda hominum illustrans! O vos, tres in personis, una vero Deitas in substantia, qui Adam et Evam in peccatis eorum pepercistis et propter corum peccata mortem subiste, Tu Filii turpissimam et in ligno sanctae crucis substinuisti, O Misericordissime, quando ad tuam confugio Misericordiam, et supplico omnibus modis quibus possim per haec nomina sancta Filii tui, scilicet Alpha et Omega, et per omnia alia sua nomina quatenus aptus me facias Genios meos complementares, Angelos omnes tuos, sive in Coelo stantes, sive de coelo ejectos, in cospectu meo invocare, evocare, citare, ut ipsi, sicut omnes intelligentiae universi mecum loquantur, ut ego possim eos in interrogare de quibus in cognoscendo potestatem omnium, et secundum statum, conditionem et potestatem corum, mandata mea perficiant sive mora, insa corum voluntate, sive aliqua laesione corporis, animae et bonorum meorum.

✠ Per Dominum nostrum Jesu Christum Filium Tuum. qui tecum vivit et regnat in unitate Spiritus Sancti Deus, per omnia saecula saeculorum, Amen ✠

(Translation)

Almighty and everlasting God, who deemed to unite your angels to be your servants and to serve you: Abraham, Hagar, Moses, Manoach, Elias, Gad, Joshua, Jacob, Gedeon, Lot, Israel, David, Josef, Zachary, Daniel, Mary of Madalena, and countless others; you who through them, have protected them, you have provided and led them to the last haven of salvation; and have brought me into eternal joy, I humbly ask you to forgive my sins, and receive this prayer with compassion and kindness, your holy angels. These things I ask, O Lord, God of Piety, God of Patience, Most Kind, Most Liberal, Most High, you who will show your accord, your gratitude, who will forgive the iniquities, sins, and crimes of men, in the sight of men, among the grandchildren, and even to the fourth generation, because I recognize my misery, and am not worthy to appear before your divine majesty, nor to implore and abhor your clemency, and your mercy for the least amount of grace. But yet, Lord of Lords, yours is a great source of your goodness, so that he himself calls those whom they are ashamed of for their sins, and invites them to receive their thanks. I implore thee, therefore, O Lord my God, to have pity on me, and take away all my wickedness and my iniquity. Cleanse my soul from all the foulness of sin, restore my spirit and comfort me so that I may be strong and able to understand the mystery of your grace, and the treasures of your wisdom. With this oil of your holiness sanctify me, as you have sanctified all your servants as slaves. By this oil, sanctify all things that are in me, that I may be worthy of Your holy angels, that I may be able to act with them, and receive information concerning them, and through them to hold dominion in Your divine wisdom. To the ever powerful and everlasting God, who hast made all creation for your glory and your honor, and not for the benefit of man, I humbly ask that you would deem to send me as my Genies or Genii, of the solar order, to restore communication and intercourse among us; so that I may know them and receive knowledge from them, that they may teach me about all that I have questioned about them, or that all the remedies which I have acquired from me may be contrary to oedema. Forgive me from cancer or any other disease. And this may be done, not by my own will, but by your will, in the name of Jesus Christ, your only Son, our Lord. Amen. Almighty and Everlasting God, Lord of heaven and earth, Creator of all things visible and invisible, I ...N...(name), Your unworthy servant, I call upon You according to Your commandment, through the name of Your Only Son, Jesus Christ Our Lord, and by the mysterious power of Your Most Holy His Name:

יהשוה (Jehosciua)

That thou wouldst not deem to send thy Holy Spirit, who would not guide me in truth to your absolute good. I do not most ardently desire dominion over the science of life, with perfect knowledge of what is necessary for me. Most obscure knowledge which cannot be penetrated without your help, grant me any one of your angels, genies or spirits, to teach me those rules of Holy Wisdom, the things that are to be learned from them in your pleasure in following and honouring you, and give my neighbour an oath to give me a teachable heart, that I may easily learn all that you are teaching me, and I will receive them in my mind, to spread them like a stream of your inexorable treasures, for all just reasons, and even grant me this grace to use these highest benefits in humble fear and fearful reverence. Almighty and eternal God, in the name of our Lord Jesus Christ, Father and Son and Holy Spirit, Holy Trinity and Inseparable Unity, I call upon you to be my salvation and defence and protection of my body and soul and the truth of all my sins. By the power of the Holy Cross and by the power of Your Passion, I beseech thee, O Lord Jesus Christ, by the merits of the Blessed Virgin Mary, your mother, and of all your saints, to grant me divine grace and power over all your holy angels, and in the spirit of the elements, and also in the malignant spirits, so that according to their state, condition, and power, whatever names I shall call or call out, assemble from every quarter immediately, and fulfill my will perfectly; and let those who minister, by your distinct virtue perceive it, fulfill my commandments. Amen.

Cadosh, Cadosh, Cadosh, The Lord God of Hosts, who will come to judge the living and the dead: you who are the First and the Last, King of Kings and Lord of the Lords, El ✠ Elohim ✠ Elche ✠ Zebaoth ✠ Elion ✠ Ascierceie ✠ Adonay ✠ Jah ✠ Tetragrammaton ✠ Shadday ✠ Ischiros ✠ Aghios ✠ Eleison Jmas ✠ Agla ✠ Messias ✠; by these your holy names and by these other things Elchim ✠ Chibor ✠ Eloha ✠ Elohim Zebaoth ✠ Ieve Zebaoth ✠ Elhay ✠ Adonay Melech ✠ By all your other names, I invoke and pray, O Lord Jesus Christ, through Your Birth and Baptism, by Your Passion and Your Cross, by Your Ascension, by the Coming of the Holy Spirit, the Comforter, through the bitterness of your soul when it came out of your body, through your five wounds, through the blood and water that had gone out of your body, By Your Virtue, by the Sacrament You gave Your Disciples on the Day of Your Passion, by the Holy Trinity, by the Individual Unity, by the Blessed Mary Thy matron, by the angels and archangels, and the prophets and patriarchs, and through all Your saints and through all the sacraments which are performed in Your honor; I worship, and I pray that you may accept these by prayer, and grant me the greatest power of all these conspiracy and all the words of my mouth, by which, as I will, through the Lord Jesus Christ, O God of our salvation, grant me your power and power over all your angels, whether standing in heaven, or coming out of heaven to deceive the human race, and over the spirits of the elements or fire, and air, and water, or fire, to draw them by the hand, to bind them, to bequeath and to loose them alike; and to assemble them before me, so that they may do as much as they can, and do not despise my words and my voice, but obey me and my sayings, and fear me. By your kindness and mercy and grace I pray, and prayer through the power, and the power of God the Father through the wisdom of the Son of the Redeemer of all men, and through the clemency of the Holy Spirit. That is, by whom he fulfilled the titanic law; who is, who was, and who will always be ✠ Almighty ✠ Aghios ✠ Iskyros ✠ Athanatos ✠ Soter ✠ Tetragrammaton ✠ Jeova ✠ Alpha and Omega, and through all Your holy things, and through all Your saints, and your saints by angels and archangels, Powers, Dominations, and Virtues; and by that name of which Solomon bound by the demon and was obeyed by him. And by El, Elohim, Elohe, Zebaoth, Elion, Eieie Ascer Eiie, Adonay, Jah, Tetragrammaton, Shadday, and all your names that are written in this book, and by the power of those words, and by virtue of which you can assemble and bind together; all your spirits, whether standing in heaven, or cast out from heaven, or spirits of the elements, so that, having asked me truthfully about all my questions about which I may seek, that they may give a truthful answer, and satisfy all my commandments, without harming my body, soul, and everything that pertains to me. Give me, Lord, the power which you have granted to your servants and prophets over all spirits, or angels, or spirits of the elements, such as Salamanders, Pygmies, Fates, Dryads, Sylvanus, Nymphs, Gnomes, Undines, and Sylphs. O Father Almighty, O Wise Son, O Holy Spirit that enlightens the hearts of men! O you, three persons, but one Godhead in substance, who spared Adam and Eve in their sins, and, on account of their sins, had undergone death, You endured the most shameful son, and on the tree of the holy cross, O Most Merciful, when I fly to Your Mercy, and I beseech you in every way by which I may be able by these holy names of your Son, namely Alpha and Omega, and by all their other names, in order that you may make me fit for my complementary genies, all your angels, whether standing in heaven, or cast out of heaven, to invoke, in my sight, to summon; so that I may be able to interrogate those of whom in knowing the power of all things, and according to their state, condition, and power, they may fulfill my commands, whether by delay, by their will or by any injury to my body, soul, and property.

Through our Lord Jesus Christ, Thy Son. God who lives and reigns with you in the unity of the Holy Spirit, forever and ever. Amen.

The Great Magical Invocation

May the name of the supreme spirit always be praised and glorified, to whom we humbly bow at this solemn hour. To you exalted Adonay, I direct my ardent prayers; I implore you to assist me, and to grant me the highest honour of sending me one of your glorious messengers, who may be of assistance to me in the sacred operations. Do not see me as an ambitious fool, but consider me, O great Adonay, the humblest of created beings, prostrate before the divine majesty; to whom I ask with anxious prayer to know, through the spirits of wisdom, a ray of his immaculate glory.

My prayer and request to all the high celestial spirits, and pray before the throne of the supreme master, deign to grant me the intercession of the angels of light, for Elhoim ✠ Iehovah ✠ Zebaoth ✠

Have mercy on me, forgive my sins, do not judge me with severe eyes, and help me to reach the necessary perfection; and make me worthy to contemplate the supreme glory. May my prayer be answered in the name of Adonay, Elhoim, Iehovah, and may your radiant light come to me in the form of a glorious messenger. May the gifts of wisdom and science be granted to me in the name of the holy name of the divine trinity; and may my heart be pure to you, through the sun, the moon, the stars and all the stars of the firmament.

Magical Pentacle[119]

---

119 TN: See *Heptameron* in the section 'Of the Garment and Pentacle'. Also, see *Grimoire of Pope Honorius* and *Grimoirium Verum*.

Great Magical Operation or Rite of Evocation of the Supreme Spirits

The evocation ceremony will not be officiated, except in the crescent moon of Aries, after no less than six months from the beginning of the first rites. In this circumstance, it will be a question of evoking one's own superior angel, to be consecrated as magus, to receive his sum and assistance to acquire dominion over the other angels, and the elemental spirits. Subsequently, with the prior consent of the superior angel, it will be possible to proceed with the evocation of the princes of the elements and their subordinates.

It is good to evoke one's own superior angel of Sunday; for all the other spirits, it is necessary to know in advance, their name and nature, possibly the number or monogram. It should be noted that the spirits of each planet must be called on the very day of the planet itself.

For the first evocation, abstain from any sacrifice to Venus, remaining in chastity for a preventive period of twenty-two days; three days will suffice for subsequent operations. In no case will one operate without being in the grace of God.

The circle is drawn according to the established rules; then holding the magical pentacle in the right, and the consecrated sword in the left; one (is to) invoke one's superior angel with great intensity, reciting the great magical Invocation three or five times, which must be followed by the invocation:

> Omnipotens Sempiterne Deus, qui creationem totam ad glorificationem at honorem tuum feciste et ad utilitatem hominis, supplex te rogo ut Angelum Custodene meum, (nelle evocazioni di altri Angeli o Geni, si indichera il nome dello Spirito voluto)[120] ad me mittere digneris, qui mihi communicet et me doceat de omnibus quae eum quaesivero, vel ut remedium quidque a me quaesitum contra hydropisiam vel alium malum me donet. Et hoc fiat non ex mea sed ex Tua voluntate, in Nomine Jesu Christi Filii Unici. Amen ✠.

(Translation)

> Almighty and everlasting God, you who made the whole creation for your glorification and your honor and for the benefit of man; I humbly ask you to send my Guardian Angel, let him share and teach me about all the things that I seek for him, whether that he may give me any remedy which I have sought against hydropsis, or some other evil. And this may be done, not of mine, but of your will, in the name of Jesus Christ the Only Son. Amen.

---

120 In the evocations of other Angels or Genii, the name of the desired Spirit will be indicated

The Great Invocation, and these senses will come. If you wish, you can recite the Christian prayer of the angel of the Lord, of perfumes that will spread out, failing to communicate with him, one will take his leave with the formula:

I give thanks to God for having sent you, and to you for having come in His name. Go back to your business in peace ready to to come when I call you, as this has been allowed to me by the Creator. Amen. ✠

Therefore, to be able to communicate with the angel, you will need a mirror or a carafe full of water, and a medium in an ecstatic condition by imposition of the hands.

For the Evocation of any other Angels or Genies

Once you enter the magic circle, recite the Great Invocation, the conjuration of the angel of the day, and the prayer 'Omnipotens Sempiterne Deus ...' given above. Call the desired angel by name, and if you have the number, write it. At the end of the interview, the operator never forgets to dismiss the genies with the formula given above.

For the Evocation of the Elemental Spirits and the Princes of the Elements

Having entered the circle, the operator recites the following prayer by himself and (then) by his assistants; after making sure of the presence of his own angel, and of those of his assistants, whom he ritually invoked. (Prayer 1).

Prayer 2

O Pater omnipotens, O Filii sapiens; O Spiritus Sancte corda hominum illustrans! O vos, tres in personis, una vero Deitas in substantia, qui Adam et Evam in peccatis corum pepercistis et propter corum neccata mortem subisti, Tu Fili horribilem, et in ligno Sanctae Crucis substinuiste. O Misericordissime, quando ad tuam confugio misericordiam, et supplico omnibus modis quibus possim, per haec nomina sancta Filii Tui, Scilicet: Alfa et Omega, et per omnia alia sua nomina, quatenus concedas mihi virtutem et potestatem tuam, ut valeam tuos spiritus qui de coelo ejecti sunt, sive spiritus elementorum, ante me citare, ut ipsi mecum loquantur et mandata mea perficiant statim et sive mora, sua sponte, sive aliqua laesione corporis, animae et bonorum meorum. Amen. ✠

(Translation)

O Almighty Father, O wise Son; O Holy Spirit enlightening the hearts of men! Oh you, three persons, but one Godhead in substance, who spared Adam and Eve of their sins, and died unburied on account of them; O Most Merciful, when I fly to Your mercy, and I beg you in every way that I may, by these holy names of Your Son, namely: Alpha and Omega, and by all their other names, in order that you may grant me your power and authority, so that I may be able to cite before me, of your spirits who were cast out of heaven, or the spirits of the elements, so that they may speak with me, and complete my commandments immediately and without delay, or from any injury to my body, soul and assets. Amen. ✠

This prayer (2) must be recited after the conjuration.

Prayer 1

To Be Recited Before the Conjuration

Omnipotens Aeterne Deus, in nomine Domini nostri Jesu Christi, Patris et Filii et Spiritus Sancti. Sancta Trinits et inseparabilis Unitas, Je invoco ut sis mihi salus et defensio, et protectio corporis et animae meae et omnium verum mearum. Per virtutem + Sanctae Crucis, et per virtutem Passionis tuae, deprecor te Domine Jesu Christi, per merita beatissimae Mariae Virginis et Matris tuae atque omnium Sanctorum Tuorum, ut mihi concedas gratiam et potestatem divinam super omnes sanctos Angelos tuos, atque in elementorum vel malignos spiritus, ut secundum statum et conditionem et potestatem corum quoscumque nominibus invocavero, statim ex omni parte conveniant, et voluntatem meam perfecte adimpleant, quod nihil nocentes mihi, neque timorem inferentes, sed potens oboedientes et ministrantes, tua distincta virtute percipientes, mandata mea perficiant. Amen.

Sanctus, Sanctus, Sanctus, Dominus Deus Sabaoth, qui venturus es judicare vivos et montuos: tu qui es primus et novissimus, Rex regum et Dominus dominantium, El ✠ Elhoim ✠ Elohe ✠ Zebaoth ✠ Elion ✠ Ascereieie ✠ Adonay ✠ Yah ✠ Tetragrammaton ✠ Shadday ✠ Ischiros ✠ Aghios ✠ Eleison Imas ✠ Agla ✠ Messias ✠ per haec tua sancta nomina, per haec: Jod ✠ Jah ✠ Jeue ✠ El ✠ Elohim Gibor ✠ Elohe ✠ Elohim Zebaoth ✠ Jeue Zebaoth ✠ Elohi ✠ Adonay Melech ✠ et per omnia alia invoco et obsecro Je Domine Jesu Christi, per nativitatem et Baptesimum Tuum, per passionem et Crucem Tuam, per Ascensionem tuam, per Edventum Spiritus Sancti Paracliti, per amaritudinem animae tuae quando exivit de corpore tuo per quinque vulnera tua per sanguinem et aquam qui exierant de corpore tuo, per Virtutem Tuam, per sacramentum quod dedisti discipulis Tuis pridie passionis Tuae, per Sanctam Trinitatem, per individuam Unitate, per Beatam Mariam Matrem Tuam, per Angelos et Archangelos, et Prophetas et Patriarchas, et per omnes Sanctos Tuos, obsecro te, benedico tibi, et rogo ut acceptes horationes has et summam potentiam dones his conjurationibus et verbis oris mei omnibus quibus uti volucro, peto Domine Jesu Christe, Deus nostrae salutis: da mihi virtutem et potestatem tuam super omnes Angelos Tuos, sive in coelo stantes, sive de coelo ejecti ad decipiendum genus humanum, et super spiritus elementorum sive terrae, et aquae, et aeris aut ignis, ad atteaendum cos, ad constringendum, ad ligandum eos pariter et solvendum et ad congragandum eos corum me, ut quae possunt faciant, et verba mea, vocemque meam nullo modo contemnant, sed mihi et dictis meis oboediant, et me timeant.

Per Dominum Nostrum Jesum Christum Filium Tuum, qui tecum vivit et regnat, in unitate spiritus Sancti Deus, per omnia saecula saeculorum. Amen ✠'

(Translation)

Almighty Eternal God, in the name of our Lord Jesus Christ, the Father and Son and Holy Spirit. The Holy Trinity and inseparable Unity, I call upon you to be my salvation and defense, and the protection of my body and soul, and the truth of all my sins. By the power ✠ of the Holy Cross and by the power of your Passion, I beseech you, O Lord Jesus Christ, through the services of the Most Blessed Virgin, your Mother and of all Your Saints, that you may grant me divine grace and power over all your holy angels, and against the elements or evil spirits; so that according to their state, condition, and authority, whatever names I shall call upon, assemble from every quarter immediately, and fulfill my will perfectly; that they may do me no harm, nor inflict fear; but mighty, obedient and ministering, receiving by your distinct prowess, to fulfill my commandments. Amen.

Holy, Holy, Holy, Lord God of Hosts, who will come to judge the living and of the mountains, you who are the first and last king of kings and lord of lords, El ✠ Elhoim ✠ Elohe ✠ Zebaoth ✠ Elion ✠ Ascereieie ✠ Adonay ✠ Yah ✠ Tetragrammaton ✠ Shadday ✠ Ischiros ✠ Aghios ✠ Eleison Imas ✠ Agla ✠ Messias ✠ by these Thy holy names, by these: Jod ✠ Jah ✠ Jeue ✠ El ✠ Elohim Gibor ✠ Elohe ✠ Elohim Zebaoth ✠ Jeue Zebaoth ✠ Elohi ✠ Adonay Melech ✠ and through all other things. I invoke and pray to Jesus Christ, through Your Birth and Baptism, through Your Passion and Your Cross, through Your Ascension, through the coming of the Holy Spirit, the Paraclete, through the bitterness of your soul, when it came out of your body through your five wounds, through your blood and water that had gone out of your body; by your Virtue, by the Sacrament, you gave to your disciples on the eve of your Passion, by the Holy Trinity, by the Individual Unity, by the Blessed Mary, Your Mother, by the Angels and Archangels, and the Prophets and Patriarchs, and by all Your Saints, I beg you, I bless you, and I ask that you accept these prayerss, and grant them the supreme power, and the words of my mouth, to all that I may fly, I beseech thee, O Lord Jesus Christ, the God of our salvation: give me thy power and power above all thy angels whether standing in heaven, or being cast out of heaven to deceive the human race, and over the spirits of the elements, of earth, and of water, and of air, or of fire, which they can do, and let them in no way despise my words and my voice, but obey me and my words, and fear me.

Through our Lord Jesus Christ, your Son, who lives and reigns with you, God in the unity of the Holy Spirit, forever and ever. Amen.

Psalm 137[121]

Confitebor tibi, Domine, in toto corde meo, quoniam audisti verba ous mei.
In cospectu angelorum psallam tibi.
Adorabo et templum sanctum tuum,
et confitebor nomini tuo super misericordia tua et veritate tua, quoniam magnificasti super omne nomen sanctum tuum.
In guacumque die invocavero te, exaudi me;
multiplicabis in anima mea virtutem.
Confiteantur tibi Domine, omnes reges terrae,
quia audirent omnia verba oris tui;
et cantent in viis Domini;
quoniam magnaest gloria Domini;
quoniam excelsus Dominus, et humilia respicit,
et alta a longe cognoscit.
Si ambulavero in medio tribulationibus, vivificabis me;
et super iram inimicorum meoum extendiste manum tuam,
et salvum me fecit dertera tua.
Dominus retribuet pro me.
Domine, misericordia tua in saeculum;
opera manum tuarum ne despicias.

---

121 TN: This is Psalm 138 in the *King James Bible*, rather than 137, and it should be noted that the numbering assigned to the 150 Psalms in the Book of Divine Worship is based on the standard Hebrew text (the Masoretic Text), therefore one number off from the classic Latin version after number 9.

(Translation)

I will confess to you, Lord, with all my heart, because you have heard the words of my prayer.
In the care of the angels I will sing to you.
I will also worship your holy temple
and I will confess to your name because of your mercy and your truth, because you have magnified your holy name above all.
In every day I call upon thee, hear me;
You will increase my strength in my soul.
Let all the kings of the earth praise you, Lord.
because they would hear all the words of your mouth;
and sing in the ways of the Lord;
since the glory of the Lord is great;
since the Lord is high, and respects the lowly,
and he knows the deep from afar.
If I walk in the midst of troubles, you will revive me;
and you have stretched out your hand upon the wrath of my enemies,
and thy mother saved me.
The Lord will repay for me.
Lord, your mercy is for ever;
do not despise the works of your own hands.

Also this psalm is dedicated to King David:

1. [A Psalm] of David. I will praise thee with my whole heart: before the gods will I sing praise unto thee.

2. I will worship toward thy holy temple, and praise thy name for thy loving kindness and for thy truth: for thou hast magnified thy word above all thy name.

3. In the day when I cried thou answeredst me, and strengthenedst me with strength in my soul.

4. All the kings of the earth shall praise thee, O Lord, when they hear the words of thy mouth.

5. Yea, they shall sing in the ways of the Lord: for great is the glory of the Lord.

6. Though the Lord be high, yet hath he respect unto the lowly: but the proud he knoweth afar off.

7. Though I walk in the midst of trouble, thou wilt revive me: thou shalt stretch forth thine hand against the wrath of mine enemies, and thy right hand shall save me.

8. The Lord will perfect that which concerneth me: thy mercy, O Lord, endureth for ever: forsake not the works of thine own hands.

Consecration of the Sword and the Magic Wand

They will consecrate the sword and the wand, (by) exposing them in the months of May and June to the rays of the moon for seven minutes on the day of the new moon, on the day of the first quarter, of the full moon of the last quarter. Then the following formula is recited:

I consecrate you, oh holy and shining instruments of the magical art, be useful to me and proposed in my operations, in the name of El, Elohim, Elohe, Zebaoth, Adonay, Shadday and for all 72 divine names.

Everything will then be perfumed with incense and camphor.[122]

Conjuration

Conjuro vos, Spiritus Elementorum, Ignis, Aeris, Aquae et terrae, et omnes immundos spiritus, sive praesentes sive absentes, vos rursus conjuro, ut quoscumque nominibus voravero vos, statim ex omni parte ad me veniates, et mihi oboediatis in omnibus, et voluntatem meam plene adimpleatis; quod mihi nihil nocentes neque timorem inferentes, sed oboedientes et submissi, mandata mea perficiatis.

Hoc vos jubeo ✠ per Maximum deum Viventem ✠ per Deum Verum ✠ per Deum Sanctum ✠ per deum Patrem ✠ per Deum Filium ✠ per deum Spiritum Sanctum, et maxim per Quem, homo factus, sicut agnus crucifixus et immolatus est, et pro ✠ Sanguine cujus, Michael Archangelus, pugnando contra vos, vos fregit et fugavit.

Vos jubeo mihi oboedientiam et submissionem integralem prae, stare, sive calliditate vel insidiis, et sive aliqua laesione, corporis, animae et bonorum meorum, nec comitum aut miunctorum meorum, ✠ per Potentiam et Virtutem Dei Patris, ✠ per Sapientiam Filii Redemptoris Omnium hominum et per clementiam Spiritus Sancti: id est ✠ per Quem Legem totam complevit ✠ Qui erat ✠ est ✠ et semper crit: ✠ Omnipotens, ✠ Aghios ✠ Ischiros ✠ Athanatos ✠ Soter ✠ Tetragrammaton ✠ Jeovah ✠ Alfa et ✠ Omega, et per omnia sancta, et per Angelos et Archangelos, Potestates, Dominationes, et virtutes, et per illud Nomen per quod Salomo constringebat daemones et oboediebatur ab ipsis.

Et per El, Aelohim, Elohe, Zebaoth, Elion, Eieie Ascer Eieie, Adonay, Jah, Shadday, et per omnia Sancta nomina quae scripta sunt in hoc libro.

---

122 TN: See Mathers, 1889, Book II, chapter VIII.

Et si vos huie jussu detrectature aut resistituri estis, Sanctus Michael Archangelus, Jusso Sanctissimae Trinitatis, vos immerget in lacu sulphuris et ignis, qui vobis paratus est.

Quia jussum hoc quod nunc vos jubeo, non oritur a me sed ab eo Ente Ineffabile qui a sinu Aeterni Patris missus est ad vos subjugandum, quod fecit mortem patendo in ligno Crucis.

Omnibus baptiratis qui credunt in Eo, dedit Ille potestatem jubendi vos, et pro gloria sua, et ad omnium utilitatem.

Impero vobis igitur ut mihi in omnia oboediatis, mihi veraciter de omnibus meis quaestionibus interrogatis, de quibus quaeram, veracem responsum tribuatis, ut omnibus mandatis meis satisfaciatis, et voluntatem meam diligenter adimpleatis.

Et hoc per signum Sanctae Crucis et per Pentaculum Magicum Salomonis.
Ecce Crucem Domini (Tracciare nell'aria il segno della Croce).
Ecce Pentaculum Salomonis (Mostrare il Pentacolo).

(Translation)

I conjure you, the Spirit of the Elements, Fire, Air, Water, and Earth, and all unclean spirits, Whether present or absent, I conjure you again, that as many as I shall call you by name, you shall immediately come to me in every quarter, and obey me in all things, and fully fulfill my will; without harming me, and inflicting no fear, but being obedient and submissive, you fulfill my commandments.

I order you by the greatest living God ✠ by the True God ✠ by God the Holy Spirit ✠ by God the Father ✠ by God the Son ✠ by God the Holy Spirit, and by whom the greatest man was made, like a lamb crucified and sacrificed; and for his blood, of Michael the Archangel fighting against you, had broken you and put you to flight.

I command you to complete obedience ad submission to me, to stand without cunning or scheming, and without injury of my body or soul or goods, nor of my companions or minions, through the mercy of the Holy Spirit, through whom he who fulfilled the whole law, who was, who is and who always speaks: ✠ Almighty, ✠ Aghios ✠ Ischiros, ✠ Athanatos, ✠ Soter, ✠ Tetragrammaton, ✠ Jeovah, ✠ Alpha, and ✠ Omega; and through all the holy things; and by angels and archangels, Powers, Dominions, and Virtues; and by that name which Solomon bound the demons, and they obeyed him.

And by El, Aelohim, Elohe, Zebaoth, Elion, Eieie, Asher, Eieie, Adonay, Jah, Shadday, and all the holy names that are written in this book.
And if you refuse or resist this order, the Archangel Saint Michael, by the order of the Most Holy Trinity, will immerse you in the pit of brimstone and fire that is prepared for you.

Because this command which I now order you does not arise from me, but from that ineffable being who was sent from the bosom of the eternal Father to subjugate you, which he did by spreading death on the tree of the cross.

To all those who have been baptized, (to those) who believe in Him; he has given me the power to command you, both for his glory and for the benefit of all.

I command you therefore that you obey me in all things, that you answer me truthfully about all my questions of which I may seek; and that you give a truthful answer; that you may satisfy all my commands, and fulfill my will diligently.

And this by the sign of the Holy Cross and by the Magical Pentacle of Solomon.
Behold the Cross of the Lord (Trace the sign of the cross in the air).
Behold the Pentacle of Solomon (Show the pentacle).

Therefore, the desired elemental spirit and their princes should be called aloud; and if they do not appear, (then) the conjuration is repeated, preceded by prayer 2.

Once the conjuration is repeated, the elementals and four princes, will present themselves. Then the operator will have each of them assign a familiar spirit, in the presence of their own superior angel; and will have the name, number and rank of the spirits which, due to their specific skills, could be useful to them in their affairs.

In any case, whether they managed to communicate with the evoked spirits, or not even perceived them present; (still) they do not leave the magic circle without having pronounced the ritual formula of reference given above; nor without having sprinkled around holy water, or water mixed with salt; because the spirits could be present even if invisible; and the operators would receive serious damage due to the strong tension released, with danger of life.

Once regular relations have been established with the spirits, when these have shown to recognise the authority of the magician, and to lend him their obedience, their evocation will no longer require the ritual apparatus described above. It will be enough to open the book to the corresponding page, trace the number, and compel the desired spirit to show itself.

This book is strictly personal and after consecration, it must be used with the utmost caution and respect, keeping it at all costs away from vulgar curiosity, and from the prying eyes of the profane; since the spirits do not like to be disturbed by those who do not have the right and the power.

To preserve its magical power intact, it is advisable to keep the book in a red silk case, on which the Seal of Solomon[123] will be embroidered in yellow.

Invocation of the Book of Spirits

In the Name of the Father, the Son and the Holy Spirit! Hasten all you spirits! For the power and virtue is sovereign; I order you, spirits of the abyss to manifest in my presence before this pentacle of King Solomon, whenever you are called! Come then, by my orders, to do what I want, within the limits of your powers! Come then, from the east, from the south, from the west and from the north! I command and invoke all of you, by the power of Him who is three in one, who is invisible, and who is eternal; the one who created the heavens, the sea, the earth and the fire!

After reciting the invocation, the ominous spirits, (are to) appear in front of the magician; then you will have to order them to sign the book with their seals, as proof and testimony of the oath, which requires them to show up whenever they are invoked.

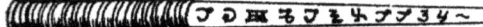

Magic Wand[124]

---

123 TN: See Crowley, 1904 for 'The Secret Seal of Solomon'.
124 TN: See, Mathers 1889, plate XIII, figure 69. Also see Book Two, Chapter VIII, 'Of the Knife, Sword, Sickle, Poniard, Dagger, Lance, Wand, Staff, and Other Instruments of Magical Art'. Mathers, 1898:77, states: 'You shall also have a wand of almond tree wood, smooth and straight, of the length of about from half an ell to six feet. And ye shall keep the aforesaid things in good order in the cupboard of the altar, ready for use in the proper time and place.'

Illustration of Michael with sigils[125]

---

125 TN: The invocations (conjurations and/or prayers) of the Days of the Week, and corresponding archangels, planets, etc. match those presented in *The Magus* derived from and matching those in the *Heptameron*.

MICHAEL[126]

Conjuro et confirmo super vos Angeli fortes Dei et sancti, in nomine Adonay, Eye, Eye, Eye, qui est ille, qui fuit est et erit, Eye, Abraye, et in nomine Saday, Cados, Cados, Cados, alte sedentis super Cherubim et per nomen magnus ipsius, Dei fortis et potentis exaltaturque, super omnes coelos, Eye, Seraye, plasmatoris saeculorum, qui creavit mundum, coelum, terram, mare et omnia, quae in us sunt in primo die, et sigillavit eo sancto nomine suo Phaa, et per nomen sanctorum angelorum, qui dominantive in quarto exercitu, et serviunt coram, potentissimo Salamia, angelo magno et honorato, et per nomen stellae, quae est sol, et per nomen Dei vivi, et per signum, et per nomina omnia praedicta, conjuro te Michael, angele magne qui es praepositus diei dominicae, et per Adonay, Dei Israel, qui creavit mundum et quid in eo est, quod pro me labores, et adimpleas omnem meam petitionem, juxta meum velle et votum meum, in negotiv et causa mea.

(Translation)

I conjure and confirm upon you, strong and holy angel of God, in the name of Adonay, Eye, Eye, Eye, who is he who was and will be, Eye, Abraham, and in the name of Saday, Cados, Cados, Cados; he who sits high over the cherubim and by his great name, the mighty and powerful God, and is exalted above all the heavens, Eye, Seraye, creator of the ages, who created the world, heaven, earth, sea, and all things that are in us on the first day; and sealed it with his holy name Phaa; and by the name of the holy angels, who are dominant in the fourth army, and serve before, the most powerful Salamia, the great and respected angel; and the name of the star, which is the sun; and the name of the living God, and the sign, and all the names mentioned above; I conjure thee, Michael, the great angel, who was appointed over the Lord's day; and by Adonay, God of Israel, who created the world and what is in it; that you worked for me and fulfilled all my requests according to my will and my desire, in my business and my interests.

---

126 TN: Michael, 'He who is as God'] In biblical and post-biblical literature, Michael is considered as the greatest of all angels, of Islamic, Jewish and Christian religions. He is the chief of the archangels, and of the order of Virtues, and ruler of the fourth heaven. From Chaldean origins, whereas he was worshiped as kind of a God. His mysterious name is Sabbathiel. In ancient Persian lore, he was known as Beshter. He is known as the Prince of Light from the *Dead Sea Scrolls*. He is also the spirit of the Sun. Archangel of Tiphereth. He is described as a king having a sceptre, riding on a lion.

Illustration of Gabriel with sigils

GABRIEL[127]

Conjuro et confirmo super vos, Angeli fortes et boni, in nomine Adonay, Adonay, Adonay, Eye, Eye, Eye, Cados, Cados, Cados, Achim, Achim, Achim, la, la, fortis la, qui apparuit in monte Sinai cum glorificatione Regis Adonay, Saday, Tsebaoth, Amathay, Ya, Ya, Ya, Marinata, Abin, Jeia, qui maria, creavit stagna et omnes aquas in secundo die, quasdam super coelos, et quasdam in terra sigillavit mare, in alto nomine suo, et terminum quem sibi posuit, non praeteribit; et per nomina angelorum qui dominantur in primo exercitu, qui serviunt Orphaniel, angelo magno pretioso et honorato; et per nomen stellae quae est in Luna, et per nomina praedicta super te conjuro scilicet, Gabriel, qui es praepositus dici Lunae secundo, quod pro me labores et adimpleas omuem meam petitionem, juxtca meum velle et votum meum, in negotio et causa mea.

(Translation)

I conjure and confirm upon you, strong and good angel, in the name of Adonay, Adonay, Adonay, Eye, Eye, Eye, Cados, Cados, Cados, Achim, Achim, Achim, la, la, Mighty God who appeared on Mount Sinai when with the glorification of the King Adonay, Saday, Tzebaoth, Amathay, Ya, Ya, Ya, Marinata, Abin, Jeia, who is Maria; who created the seas and all the waters on the second day, some above the heavens, and some on the earth sealed by the sea on the horizon; by his name, and the limit which he has set for himself, it will not pass away; and by the names of the angels who rule in the first army, who serve Orphaniel, the great, most precious and respected angel; and by the name of the star that is in the moon; and by the names mentioned above, I conjure you Gabriel, you who are appointed to be called on the second (day) Monday, because you have worked for me, and fulfilled my every request, according to my will and my desire, in my business and my cause.

---

127 TN: Gabriel, 'He is my Strength'. The second greatest of all angels after Michael, he presides over Paradise and is said to be the ruling prince of the first heaven, sitting on the left hand side of God. He is the spirit of truth, according to Mohhamed. Gabriel was credited with the destruction of Sodom and Gommorah, and also known as the prince of justice. In *Paradise Lost*, he is the chief of the angelic guards over Paradise. Also, he is said to be the 'dark antagonist' who wrestled with Jacob at Peniel, although others including Michael, Uriel and Samael have also been noted as being so. According to Babylonian legend, Gabriel fell into disgrace with God for not obeying a command exactly as given, and remained outside the 'heavenly curtain' for some time. Archangel of Yesod. He is described as a King like an archer, riding upon a doe.

Illustration of Samael with sigils

SAMAEL[128]

Conjuro et confirmo super vos Angeli fortes et sancti, per nomen Ya, Ya, Ya, He, He, He, Va, Hy, Ha, Ha, Va, Va, An, An, An, Aie, Aie, Aie, El, Ay, Elibra, Elohim, Elohim; et per nomina ipsius alti Dei, qui fecit aquam aridam apparere et vocavit terram, et produxit arbores et herbas de ea el sigillavit super eam cum pretioso, honorato, metuendo et sancto nomine suo; et per nomen angelorum, dominantium in quinto exercitu, qui serviunt Acimoy angelo magno, forti, potenti et honorato et per nomen stellae quae est Mars; et per nomina praedicta conjuro super te, Samael, angele magne qui praepositus ei diei martis, et per nomina Adonay, Dei vivi et veri, quod pro me labores et adimpleas omem meam petitionem, juxcta meum velle et votum meum, in negotio et causa mea.

(Translation)

I conjure and confirm upon you, strong and holy angel, in the name of Ya, Ya, Ya, He, He, He, He, Va, Hy, Ha, Ha, Va, Va, An, An, An, Aie, Aie, Aie, El, Ay, Elibra, Elohim, Elohim, and by the names of the High God Himself, who made the water appear dry, and called upon the earth, and produced trees and plants of it; and by the name of the angels, of the rulers in the fifth army, who serve the great angel Acimoy, the strong, powerful, and respected, and by the name of the star which is Mars; and by the aforesaid names, I conjure over you, Samael, the great angel who presided over the day of Tuesday, and by the names of Adonay, the living and true God, that you worked hard for me and fulfilled every request, according to my will and my desire, in my business and my interests.

---

128 TN: Samael, 'He who sees God' is one of the seven archangels who stand in the presence of God. Samael, or Khamael, is a warrior who represents divine justice and is the head of the angelic order of the Seraphim. In Qabalah he is the archangel of Geburah. He is described as a King, armed and riding on a wolf.

Illustration of Raphael with sigils

RAPHAEL[129]

Conjuro et confirmo vos, Angeli fortes sancti et potentes, in nomine fortis metuendissimi et benedicti Adonay, Elohim, Saday, Saday, Saday, Eye, Eye, Eye, Asamie, Asarie; et in nomine Adonay, Dei Israel, qui creavit luminaria magna ad distinquendum diem a nocte; et per nomen omnium angelorum deservientium in exercitu secundo coram terra angelo magori, atque forti et potenti; et per nomen stellae, quae est Mercurius et per nomen sigilli, quo sigillatur a Deo fortissimo et honorato, praedicta super, te, Raphael, angele magne, conjuro, qui es praepositus die quartae; et per nomen sanctum quod est scriptum in fronte Aaron, sacerdotis altissimi creatoris; et per nomina angelorum, qui in gratiam Salvatoris confirmati sunt, et per nomen sedis animalium habeinium senas alas, quod pro me labores et adimpleas omem meam petitionem, juxcta meum velle et votum meum in negotio et causa mea.

(Translation)

I conjure and confirm upon you, strong holy and powerful angel, in the name of the most formidable and blessed, of Adonay, Elohim, Saday, Saday, Saday, Eye, Eye, Eye, Asamie, Asarie; and in the name of Adonay, the God of Israel, who created great light to distinguish day from night; and by the name of all the angels who serve in the second army before the earth; the angel of the Magi, and the mighty and powerful; and by the name of the star, which is Mercury, and by the name of the seal, by which is sealed by the most powerful and honorable God, I conjure you, Raphael, the great angel, who was appointed over the fourth day; and by the holy name which is written on the forehead of Aaron, the priest of the Most High Creator; and by the names of the angels who have been confirmed in the grace of the Saviour; and by the name of the throne of animals (which) have six wings, which for me toil and fulfill all my petition, according to my will and my desire in my business and my cause.

---

129 TN: Raphael, 'Healer of God'. The third greatest angel of post-Biblical literature, derived from Chaldean lore. First appearing in the Book Of Tobit, where he acts as a guide and companion of Tobias, Tobit's son, on his journey from Nineveh. In the Book Of Enoch, he is a guide in the underworld (Sheol) and declared as one of the 'watchers'. In the Zohar he is charged to heal the earth, and through him the earth furnishes and abode for man. Also, in the Book Of Noah, he is given credit for handing the Book Of Raziel to Noah after the flood, described as a 'medical book'. He is said to be the governor of the south, guardian of the west, and ruling prince of the second heaven, overseer of the evening winds, and guardian of the Tree Of Life in the Garden of Eden. Archangel of Hod. He is described as a King riding upon a bear.

Illustration of Sachiel with sigils

SACHIEL[130]

Giovedì ♃

Conjuro et confirmo super vos, Angeli sancti, per nomen Cados, Cados, Cados, Eschereie, Eschereie, Eschereie, Hatim, Hatim, Ya, Fortis firmatus saeculorum, Cantine, Jaym, Janie, Anie, Calbar, Sabbac, Betifay, Aluaym, et per nomen Adonay, qui creavit pisces, reptilia in aquis, et aves super faciem terrae, volantes versus coelos die quinto, et per nomina Angelorum servientium in sexto exercitu coram pastore angelo sancto et maguo et potenti principe; et per nomen stellae quae est Jupiter; et per nomen sigilli sui; et per nomen Adonay, summi Dei omnium creatoris; et per nomen omnium stellarum et per vim et virtutem eaxum; et per nomina praedicta, conjuro te Sachiel, Angele magne, qui es praepositus die Jovis, quod pro me labores et adimpleas omnem meam petitionem, juxta meum velle et votum meum, in negotio el causa mea.

(Translation)

I conjure and confirm upon you, holy Angel, by the names Cados, Cados, Cados, Eschereie, Eschereie, Eschereie, Hatim, Hatim, Ya, strong, strengthened by the ages, Cantine, Jaym, Janie, Anie, Calbar, Sabbac, Betifay, Aluaym, by the name of Adonay, who created fish, creeping things in the waters, and birds on the face of the earth, flying toward the heavens on the fifth day; and the names of the angels serving in the sixth army before the holy angel, the great shepherd, and the powerful prince; and by the name of the star which is Jupiter; and by the name of his seal; and by the name of Adonay, the supreme God, creator of all; and by the name of all the stars, and by the force and power of them; And by the names mentioned above, I conjure you, Sachiel, the great angel, who was appointed on Thursday, that you worked for me and fulfilled all my request, according to my will and my desire, in my business and my cause.

---

130 TN: Sachiel, 'Covering of God', also 'water angel'. A presiding spirit of Jupiter, and resident of the first heaven, he is of the order of Cherubim, and invoked from the south. He is described as a King with sword drawn, riding on a stag.

Illustration of Anael with sigils

ANAEL[131]

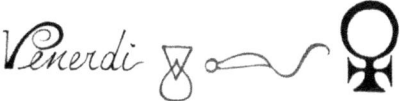

Conjuro et confirmo super vos, Angeli fortes sancti atque potentes, in nomine On, Hey, Heya, Ia, Ie, Adonay, Saday, et in nomine Saday, qui creavit quadrupedia et animalia reptilia et hominis in sexto die et Adamae dedit potestamen super omnia animalia; inde benedictum sit nomen creatoris in loco suo; et per nomina Angelorum servientium in tertio exercitu, coram Agiel, Angelo magno, principe forte atque potenti; et per nomen stellae, quae est Venus, et per sigillum ejus quod quidem est sanctum; et per nomina praedicta conjuro super te, Anael, qui es praepositus diei sextae, ut pro me labores et adimpleas omnem meam petitionem, juxta meum velle et votum meum, in negotio et causa mea.

(Translation)

I conjure and confirm upon you, strong and powerful holy angel, in the name of On, Hey, Heya, Ia, Ie, Adonay, Saday, and in the name of Saday, who created four-footed animals and reptiles, and man on the sixth day; and gave Adam power over all animals, hence blessed is the name of the Creator in its place; and by the names of the angels serving in the third army, before Agiel,[132] the great angel, a strong and powerful leader; and by the name of the star, which is Venus, and by the seal of that which is holy; and by the aforesaid names, I conjure you, Anael, who is in charge of the sixth day, that you may labor for me, and fulfill all my petition, according to my will and my desire, in my business and cause.

---

131 TN: Haniel, Anael, 'Grace of God'. A prince of the archangels, chief of the order of Principalities, and of the orders of innocents and virtues, also he holds dominion over the planet Venus and is governor of the sign Capricorn, and of the second heaven. His name is also equated with Aniel, Simiel and Onoel. Archangel of Netzach. He is described as a King with a scepte,e riding on a camel.

132 TN: Agiel is the intelligence presiding over the planet Saturn.

Cassiel

Illustration of Cassiel

CASSIEL (ZAPHKIEL)[133]

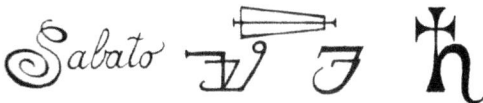

Conjuro et confirmo super vos, Caphriel vel Cassiel Machatori et Saraquiel, Angeli fortes et potentes, et per nomen Adonay, Adonay, Eye, Eye, Eye, Acim, Acim, Acim, Cados, Cados, Cados, Ia vel Ima Ima, Saday, IA, Sar, Domini, formatoris saeculorum, qui in septimo die quievit, et per illum qui in beneplacito suo filus Israel in haereditatem observandum dedit, ut eum firmiter custodirent et sanctificarent ad habendam inde bonam in alio saeculo remunerationem; et per nomina Angelorum servientium in exercitu septimo Boel Angelo magno et potenti principi; et per nomen stellae Saturnus; et per sanctum sigillum ejus; et per nomina praedicta super, conjuro te, Caphriel, qui praepositus es diei septimae, quae est dies Sabbati, quod pro me labores et adimpleas omnem meam petitionem, juxta meum velle et votum meum, in negotio et causa mea.

(Translation)

I conjure and confirm upon you, Caphriel or Cassiel, Machatori and Saraquiel, strong and powerful angel, and by the name of Adonay, Adonay, Eye, Eye, Eye, Acim, Acim, Acim, Cados, Cados, Cados, Ia or Ima Ima, Saday, IA, Sar, Domini, the former of the ages, who rested on the seventh day; and by him who in his good pleasure, gave the son of Israel an inheritance which should be observed, that they might keep him firmly and sanctify him, so as to obtain good recompense from him in another world; and by the names of the angels serving in the army of the seventh angel Boel[134] the great and powerful prince; and by the name of the star Saturn; and by his holy seal and by the names aforesaid above, I conjure you, Caphriel[135], who is in charge of the seventh day, which is the day of the Sabbath; that you worked for me and fulfilled all my requests, according to my will and my desire, of my business and my cause.

---

133 TN: Cassiel, 'Speed of God'. The angel of solitude and tears, and one of the rulers of the planet Saturn, ruling prince of the seventh heaven and prince of the order of Powers. His sigil is presented in *The Magus* by Francise Barrett, with the caption 'Specimen of the Book of Spirits, pictured riding a dragon, with an arrow in his right hand'. Also, Zaphkiel 'Knowledge of God', chief of the order of thrones and one of the nine angels that rule over Heaven.

134 TN: Boel, Boul or Bohel, It is said he holds the four keys to the four corners of the earth, which he may also unlock the gates to the paradise of Eden.

135 TN: Also see Barrett, 1801, Book II.

Formula of Evocation of the Spirits of the Book

Exorcism of Command

I summon and command you, spirit of the kingdom of shadows, to accept this magical book, made according to the art and charged with power; and to rush and appear when you are ordered, in a pleasant and not in a fearful form, as lights of the firmament.

And in no way will you harass the reader, both in his body and in his soul; and in his spirit, provoking storms, noises, confusions or disorders of any kind; and in a similar way disturbing anyone who may be with him. I summon and command you, so that you will immediately show when you will be invoked; and carry out my orders with solicitude. You will obey, you will serve, you will answer, and will carry out my will, within the limits of the power that has been granted to you; and you will do everything entirely, without deceit or false illusions; and for this no compensation will be granted to you.

If for serious reason, some of the invoked spirits should be unable to come when their presence is inquired, they will have to send other spirits, who can act on their behalf; and these too will establish with a solemn oath to carry out their will in good; of who reads the book: In virtue of the most holy names of the most holy living God: Elohim, Jah, El, Eloy, Tetragrammaton! And all of you will do everything promptly and exactly as directed.
Amen.

At the end of this last prayer, the *Book of Shadows* (*Liber Umbrarum*) is ready for use. May the magician practice it with royal wisdom, since the divine law exists above the laws of man; and glory be eternally rendered to the supreme Lord in the high heaven.

King Solomon

FINIS

Appendix A

Exorcism of Water, Prayers of the Elements, Conjuration of the Four, and Qabalistic Prayer of Solomon from *Transcendental Magic* by Eliphas Levi

Exorcism of Water

Let there be a firmament in the midst of the waters, and let it divide the waters from the waters; the things which are above are like unto things which arc below, and things below arc like unto things above, for the performance of the wonders of one thing; The sun is its father, the moon its mother, the wind hath carried it in the belly thereof. It ascendeth from earth to heaven, and again it descendeth from heaven to earth. I exorcise thee, creature of water, that thou mayest become unto men a mirror of the living God in His works, a fount of life and ablution of sins.

Prayer of the Salamanders (fire)

Immortal, Eternal, Ineffable and Uncreated Father of All, borne upon the Chariot of Worlds, which ever roll in ceaseless motion; Ruler over the Ethereal Vastness, where the Throne of Thy Power is upraised, from the summit of which Thine eyes behold all, and Thy pure and Holy ears hear all, hear Thou Thy children, whom thou hast loved since before the Ages began. Thy Majesty Golden, Vast and Eternal, shineth above the Heaven of Stars! Above them art Thou exalted, O Thou Flashing Fire! There Thou illuminateth all things with Thine insupportable Glory, whence flow the ceaseless streams of splendor which nourish thine Infinite Spirit. This Infinite Spirit nourisheth all, and maketh that inexhaustable treasure of generation which ever encompasseth Thee, replete with the numberless forms wherewith Thou hast filled it from the beginning. From this Spirit arise those most Holy Kings, who surround thy Throne and who compose Thy court. O Universal Father! One and Alone! Father alike of Immortals and of Mortals! Thou hast created Powers marvellously like unto Thy thought Eternal and unto Thy venerable Essence. Thou hast estab lished them above the Angels who announce Thy Will to the World. Lastly, thou hast created us third in rank within our Elemental Empire! There our continual exercise is to praise and to adore Thy desires! There we ceaselessly burn with Eternal Aspiration unto Thee! O Father! O Mother of Mothers, O Archetype Eternal of Maternity and of Love! O Son, the flower of all Sons! O form of all forms, Soul, Spirit, Harmony and Numeral of all Things! Amen.[136]

---

136 TN: In footnote, Waite states "This prayer is found in 'Le Comte de Gabalis: first published in 1680."

Prayer of the Sylphs (air)

Spirit of Light, Spirit of Wisdom whose breath giveth forth and withdraweth the form of all living things; Thou, before whom the Life of Beings is but a shadow which changeth, and a vapour which passeth; Thou who mountest upon the clouds, and who walketh upon the wings of the wind; Thou who breathest forth, and endless Space is peopled; Thou who drawest in Thy breath and all that cometh from Thee returneth unto Thee; ceaseless Movement in Eternal Stability, Be Thou eternally blessed! We praise Thee and we bless Thee in the changing Empire of created Light, of Shades, of reflections, and of Images and we aspire without cessation unto Thy immutable and imperishable brilliance. Let the Ray of Thine Intelligence and the warmth of Thy Love penetrate even unto us; then that which is volatile shall be fixed, the shadow shall be a body, the Spirit of Air shall be a soul, the dream shall be a thought. And no longer shall we be swept away by the Tempest, but we shall hold the bridles of the Winged Steeds of Dawn, and we shall direct the course of the Evening Breeze to fly before Thee. O Spirit of Spirits, O Eternal Soul of Souls, O imperish able breath of Life, O Creative Sigh, O mouth which breathest forth and withdrawest the Life of all Beings in the Flux and Reflux ebb and flow of thine Eternal Word which is the Divine Ocean of Movement and of Truth. Amen.

Prayer of the Undines (water)

Dread King of the Sea, who hast the Keys of the floodgates of Heaven and who enclosest the subterranean Waters in the cavernous hollows of Earth; King of the Deluge and of the Rains of Spring; Thou who openest the sources of Rivers and of Fountains; Thou who commandest moisture, which is like the blood of the earth, to become the sap of plants: We adore thee and we invoke thee! Speak thou unto us Thy inconstant and changeful creatures in the great Tempests of the Sea, and we shall tremble before Thee. Speak unto us also in the murmur of limpid waters, and we shall desire thy love. O Vastness wherein all the Rivers of Being seek to lose themselves, which renew themselves ever in thee. O Ocean of infinite perfections! O Height which reflectest Thyself in the Depth! O Depth which exhalest thyself into the Height! Lead us into Immortality through sacrifice, that we may be found worthy one day to offer unto Thee the Water, the Blood, and the Tears, for the remission of Sins! Amen.

Prayer of the Gnomes (earth)

O Invisible King Who, taking the Earth for Foundation, didst hollow its depths to fill them with Thy Almighty Power. Thou Whose Name shaketh the Arches of the World! Thou who causest the Seven Metals to flow through the veins of the rocks! King of the Seven Lights! Rewarder of the subterranean Workers! Lead us into the desirable Air and into the Realm of Splendor. We watch and we labor unceasingly, we seek and we hope, by the twelve stones of the Holy City, by the buried Talismans, by the Axis of the Lodestone which passes through the center of the Earth. O Lord, O Lord, O Lord! Have pity upon those who suffer. Expand our hearts, detach and upraise our minds, enlarge our natures. O Stability and Motion! O Darkness veiled in Brilliance! O Day clothed in Night! O Master who never dost withhold the wages of Thy Workmen! O Silver Whiteness! O Golden Splendor! O Crown of Living and Melodious Diamond! Thou who wearest the Heavens on Thy Finger like a ring of Sapphire! Thou who hidest beneath the Earth in the Kingdom of Gems, the marvelous Seed of the Stars! Live, reign, and be Thou the Eternal Dispenser of the Treasures whereof Thou hast made us the Warders! Amen.

Conjuration of the Four

Caput mortuum, the Lord command thee by the living and votive serpent! Cherub, the Lord command thee by Adam Jotchabah! Wandering Eagle, the Lord command thee by the wings of the Bull! Serpent, the Lord Tetragrammaton command thee by the angel and the lion! Michael, Gabriel, Raphael, and Anael! Flow Moisture, by the spirit of Eloim. Earth, be established by Adam Jotchabah. Spread, Firmament, by Jahubehu, Zebaoth. Fulfil, Judgment, by fire in the virtue of Michael. Angel of the blind eyes, obey, or pass away with this holy water! Work, Winged Bull, or revert to the earth, unless thou wilt that I should pierce thee with this sword! Chained Eagle, obey my sign, or fly before this breathing! Writhing Serpent, crawl at my feet, or be tortured by the sacred fire and give way before the perfumes that I burn in it! Water, return to water; fire, burn; air, circulate; earth, revert to earth, by virtue of the Pentagram, which is the Morning Star, and by the name of the Tetragram, which is written in the center of the Cross of Light! Amen.'

Qabalistic Invocation of Solomon

Powers of the Kingdom, be beneath my left foot, and within my right hand. Glory and Eternity touch my shoulders, and guide me in the Paths of Victory. Mercy and justice be ye the Equilibrium and splendour of my life. Understanding and Wisdom give unto me the Crown. Spirits of Malkuth conduct me between the two columns whereon is supported the whole edifice of the Temple. Angels of Netzach and of Hod strengthen me upon the Cubical Stone of Yesod. O GEDULAHEL! O GEBURAHEL! O TIPHERETH! BINAHEL, be Thou my Love! RUACH CHOKMAHEL, be Thou my Light! Be that which Thou art, and that which thou willest to be, O KETHERIEL! Ishim, assist me in the Name Of SHADDAL Cherubim, be my strength in the Name of ADONAL Beni Elohim, be ye my brethren in the Name of the Son, and by the virtues of TZABAOTH. Elohim, fight for me in the Name of TETRAGRAMMATON. Malachim, protect me in the Name of YOD HE VAU HE. Seraphim, purify my love in the Name of ELOAH. Chaschmalim, enlighten me with the splendours of ELOHI, and of SCHECHINAH. Aralim, act ye; Auphanim, revolve and shine. Chaioth Ha-Qadosch, cry aloud, speak, roar, and groan; Qadosch, Qadosch, Qadosch., SHADDAI, ADONAI, YOD CHAVAH, EHEIEH ASHER EHEIEH! Halelu-Yah! Halelu-Yah! Halelu-Yah. Amen.

Appendix B

Consecration of the Book, from the *Key of Solomon*

Make a small Book containing the Prayers for all the Operations, the Names of the Angels in the form of Litanies, their Seals and Characters; the which being done thou shalt consecrate the same unto God and unto the pure Spirits in the manner following:

Thou shalt set in the destined place a small table covered with a white cloth, whereon thou shalt lay the Book opened at the Great Pentacle which should be drawn on the first leaf of the said Book; and having kindled a lamp which should be suspended above the centre of the table, thou shalt surround the said table with a white curtain; clothe thyself in the proper vestments, and holding the Book open, repeat upon thy knees the following prayer with great humility:

For the Prayer beginning 'Adonai Elohim,' etc., see Book I., Chapter XIV (which is presented here):

ADONAI, ELOHIM, EL, EHEIEH ASHER EHEIEH, Prince of Princes, Existence of Existences, have mercy upon me, and cast Thine eyes upon Thy Servant (N.), who invokes Thee most devoutedly, and supplicates Thee by Thy Holy and tremendous Name Tetragrammaton to be propitious, and to order Thine Angels and Spirits to come and take up their abode in this place; O ye Angels and Spirits of the Stars, O all ye Angels and Elementary Spirits, O all ye Spirits present before the Face of God, I the Minister and faithful Servant of the Most High conjure ye, let God Himself, the Existence of Existences, conjure ye to come and be present at this Operation, I, the Servant of God, most humbly entreat ye. Amen.

Having then caused the workmen to fill in the hole, thou shalt license the Spirits to depart, thanking them for the favour they have shown unto thee, and saying:

THE LICENSE TO DEPART: O ye good and happy Spirits, we thank ye for the benefits which we have just received from your liberal bounty; depart ye in peace to govern the Element which God hath destined for your habitation. Amen.

After which thou shalt incense it with the incense proper to the Planet and the day, and thou shalt replace the Book on the aforesaid Table, taking heed that the fire of the lamp be kept up continually during the operation, and keeping the curtains closed. Repeat the same ceremony for seven days, beginning with

Saturday, and perfuming the Book each day with the Incense proper to the Planet ruling the day and hour, and taking heed that the lamp shall burn both day and night; after the which thou shalt shut up the Book in a small drawer under the table, made expressly for it, until thou shalt have occasion to use it; and every time that thou wishest to use it, clothe thyself with thy vestments, kindle the lamp, and repeat upon thy knees the aforesaid prayer, 'Adonai Elohim,' etc.

It is necessary also, in the Consecration of the Book, to summon all the Angels whose Names are written therein in the form of Litanies, the which thou shalt do with devotion; and even if the Angels and Spirits appear not in the Consecration of the Book, be not thou astonished thereat, seeing that they are of a pure nature, and consequently have much difficulty in familiarising themselves with men who are inconstant and impure, but the Ceremonies and Characters being correctly carried out devoutedly and with perseverance, they will be constrained to come, and it will at length happen that at thy first invocation thou wilt be able to see and communicate with them. But I advise thee to undertake nothing unclean or impure, for then thy importunity, far from attracting them, will only serve to chase them from thee; and it will be thereafter exceedingly difficult for thee to attract them for use for pure ends.

Appendix C

Some Pertinent Information from the *Veritable Key of Solomon*[137]

Saturday – planet Saturn – the Angel is Cassiel, the name of the familiar spirit is Arathron, the mystical number is 15.

Perfume for Saturday – a black poppy seed, henbane seed, root of mandrake, powdered magnetic stone and good quality myrrh in powder. Grind up all these herbs and mix them with the blood of a bat and the brain of a black cat.

Friday – planet Venus – the Angel is Anael, the name of the familiar spirit is Agith, the mystical number is 175.

Perfume for Friday – Musk, ambergris, aloe wood, dried red roses, red coral, having ground all this into a paste, with the blood of a dove or of turtledove, and with the brain of two or three sparrows.

Thursday – planet Jupiter – the Angel is Sachiel, the name of the familiar spirit is Bethor, the mystical number is 34.

Perfume for Thursday – Rowan berry, wood of aloes, storax, benzoin, powder of lapis lazuli, pieces of chopped up peacock feather, ground up and mixed with the blood of two or three swallows or the brain of a deer.

Wednesday – planet Mercury – the Angel is Raphael, the name of the familiar spirit is Ophiel, the mystical number is 260.

Perfume for Wednesday – Oriental mastic, any incense of choice, cloves, pentaphylla flowers, powder of agate, ground up and mixed with the brain of a fox and the blood of a magpie.

Tuesday – planet Mars – the Angel is Samael, the name of the familiar spirit is Phaleg, the mystical number is 65.

Perfume for Tuesday – Euphorbia, belladonna, ammonia salt, roots from two hellebores, powder of magnetized stone and a small amount of sulfur, ground up into a powder and mixed with the blood of a black cat and the brain of a crow.

Monday – planet moon – the Angel is Gabriel, the name of the familiar spirit is Phul, the mystical number is 369.

Perfume for Monday – dried frog's head and bull's eyes, a white poppy seed,

---

[137] Skinner & Rankine, 2008.

the most exquisite incense and a small amount of camphor, ground up and making a paste with the blood of a gosling or of a turtledove.

Sunday – planet sun – the Angel is Michael, the name of the familiar spirit is Och, and the mystical number is 111.

Perfume for Sunday – saffron, amber, musk, aloe wood, balm wood, laurel seeds, cloves, myrrh, and incense, these herbs should all be a sixth of an ounce, with the exception of the amber and musk, which should only be a grain of each. Mix all together and add some brain of eagle or some blood of a white cockerel.

Appendix D

Liber Spirituum, from *Fourth Book of Occult Philosophy* attributed to Henry Cornelius Agrippa, in the first section entitled 'Of Occult Philosophy or Of Magical Ceremonies'

THE LIBER SPIRITUUM OR BOOK OF SPIRITS

There is extant amongst those Magicians (who do most use the ministery of evil spirits) a certain Rite of invocating spirits by a Book to be consecrated before to that purpose; which is properly called, A book of Spirits (Liber Spirituum); whereof we shall now speak a few words. For this Book is to be consecrated, a book of evil spirits, ceremoniously to be composed, in their name and order: whereunto they binde with a certain holy Oath, the ready and present obedience of the spirits therein written.

Now this book is to be made of most pure and clean paper, that hath never been used before; which many do call Virgin-paper. And this book must be inscribed after this maner: that is to say, Let there be placed on the left side the image of the spirit, and on the right side his character, with the Oath above it, containing the name of the spirit, and his dignity and place, with his office and power. Yet very many do compose this book otherwise, omitting the characters or image: but it is more efficacious not to neglect any thing which conduceth to it.

Moreover, there is to be observed the circumstances of places, times, hours, according to the Stars which these spirits are under, and are seen to agree unto, their site, rite, and order being applied.

Which book being so written, and well bound, is to be adorned, garnished, and kept secure, with Registers and Seals, lest it should happen after the consecration to open in some place not intented [sic], and indanger [endanger] the operator. Furthermore, this book ought to be kept as reverently as may be: for irreverence of minde causeth it to lose its vertue, with pollution and profanation.

Now this sacred book being this composed according to the maner already delivered, we are then to proceed to the consecration thereof after a twofold way: one whereof is, That all and singular the spirits who are written in the book, be called to the Circle, according to the Rites and Order which we have before taught; and the book that is to be consecrated, let there be placed without the Circle in a triangle. And in the first place, let there be read in the presence of the spirits all the Oathes which are written in that book; and then the book to be consecrated being placed without the Circle in a triangle there drawn, let all the spirits be compelled to impose their hands where their images and characters are drawn, and to confirm and consecrate the same with a special and common Oath. Which being done, let the book be taken and shut, and preserved as we have before spoken, and let the spirits be licensed to depart, according to due rite and order.

There is another maner of consecrating a book of spirits, which is more easie, and of much efficacie to produce every effect, except that in opening this book the spirits do not always come visible. And this way is thus: Let there be made a book of spirits as we have before set forth; but in the end thereof let there be written Invocations and Bonds, and strong Conjurations, wherewith every spirit may be bound. Then this book must be bound between two Tables or Lamens, and in the inside thereof let there be drawn the holy Pentacles of the Divine Majestie, which we have before set forth and described out of the Apocalypse: then let the first of them be placed in the beginning of the book, and the second at the end of the same.

This book being perfected after this maner, let it be brought in a clear and fair time, to a Circle prepared in a cros way, according to the Art which we have before delivered; and there in the first place the book being opened, let it be consecrated to the rites and ways which we have before declared concerning Consecration. Which being done, let all the spirits be called which are written in the book, in their own order and place, by conjuring them thrice by the bonds described in the book, that they come unto that place within the space of three days, to assure their obedience, and confirm the same, to the book so to be consecrated. Then let the book be wrapped up in clean linen, and buried in the middle of the Circle, and there fast stopped up: and then the Circle being destroyed, after the spirits are licensed, depart before the rising of the sun.

And on the third day, about the middle of the night, return, and new make the Circle, and with bended knees make prayer and giving thanks unto God, and let a precious perfume be made, and open the hole, and take out the book; and so let it be kept, not opening the same. Then you shall license the spirits in their order, and destroying the Circle, depart before the sun rise. And this is the last rite and maner of consecrating, profitable to whatsoever writings and experiments, which do direct to spirits, placing the same between two holy Lamens or Pentacles, as before is shewn.

But the Operator, when he would work by the book thus consecrated, let him do it in a fair and clear season, when the spirits are least troubled; and let him place himself towards the region of the spirits. Then let him open the book under a due Register; let him invoke the spirits by their Oath there described and confirmed, and by the name of their character and image, to that purpose which you desire: and, if there be need, conjure them by the bonds placed in the end of the book. And having attained your desired effect, then you shall license the spirits to depart.

Appendix E

Prayers from 'Preghiera per la Fratellanza Ermetica',[138] from Caliel's, *Il Sacramentario Segreto*.

FORMULA PRO ABLUTIONE

Fiat firmamentum in medio aquarum et separet aqua ab aquis; et quae inferius sicut quae superius, ad perpetranda miracula rei unius. Sol ejus Pater est; Luna Mater, et ventum eam gestavit in utero suo; ascendit a terra ad coelum, et rursus a Coelo in Terram discendit. Exorciso te, creatura aquae, ut sis mihi speculum Dei vivi in operibus ejus, et, fons Vitae et ablutio peccatorum atque aurarum inquinatarum quas absorpi, nec non cupiditatum passionum et praevaricationum

(Translation)

FORMULA FOR ABLUTION[139]

Let there be a firmament in the midst of the waters, and separate the water from the waters; and what is below as well as what is above, to perform the miracles of one thing. The sun is his Father; Mother Moon, and the wind bore her in her womb; ascends from earth to heaven, and again descends from heaven to earth. I exorcise you, creature of water, that you may be for me a mirror of the living God in his works, and, a source of Life and a wash of the sins and polluted airs that I have absorbed, as well as of passions and transgressions.

ORATIO PRO INFIRMIS

Per vertutem Tuam: sanet eos Spiritus Tuum Sanitatis; Angelus Roboris Tuum restauret eos; desperdantur Spiritus infirmitatis, triumphet ... in felicitate pauperorum et afflictorum qui reccurunt ad te.

---

138 TN: 'Prayer for the Hermetic Brotherhood'

139 TN: Note parts of this (from 'what is below .... Heaven to earth') are clearly drawn from the Emerald Tablet.

(Translation)

PRAYER FOR THE SICK

Through Thy righteousness: let Thy Spirit of Healing heal them; the angel of your strength will restore them; let the spirit of weakness be wasted, triumph ... in the happiness of the poor and afflicted who have recourse to thee.

ORATIO PRO FRATERNITATE VEL ECCLESIA

Oramus pro Sancta Fraternitate Hermetica ..... Aeterne Pater; hoc rogamus et petimus, ut servi Tui (in aso di preghiera colletiva qui si aggiungera ; hic conventi) totae Nostrae Fraternitatis, semper stricte collecti sint per vinculum indissolubile Amoris, neo unquam permittes seperataturos quos Virtus junxit constitutione Familiae Unae, et ut qi in uno Templo recepti, in perpetuum maneant in eo sub ducto Tuo, nec mors separet eos.

... ne Duc invisibilis Ejus nos Derelinquat; ut Corpus Misticum Invisibile Ejus magnificetur et fortificetur, ut potentia Angeli Fortitudinis Ejus ... expandatur et miultiplicetur usque et instaurationem et confirmationem Sancti Regni; ut Angelus Ejus Rigoris ... continue factus sit justior et terribilior cum Angelus Clementiea ... suavior ac omnipraesentior semper fiat, et ut Dux Visibilis Ejus, vim habeat et virtutem ad operandum indefesse pro diffusione Sanctae Scientiae et Artis Magneticae et Magiae Aeonicae ad instaurationem Sancti Imperri in Orbi Universo; ne Providentia Coeli derelinquat nos nec infirmo nostros; ut inter nos causam pauperorum et afflictorum nemo prodeat, vilipendat aut prevaricet; ut Amor Boni colligat omnes Fratres in uno vinculo indissolubili purissimi Amoris. Amen.

(Translation)

PRAYER FOR THE FRATERNITY OF THE CHURCH

We pray for the Holy Hermetic Brotherhood ..... Eternal Father; this we ask and request, that Your servants (in case of collective prayer here is added; the respondents here) of all Our Fraternity, may always be strictly gathered together by the unbreakable bond of Love, that You may never allow to separate those whom Virtue joined by the constitution of the One Family, and as received in one Temple, may they remain in it forever under your guidance, and death shall not separate them.

... let not His invisible Guide forsake us; that His Invisible Mystical Body may be magnified and strengthened, that the power of His Angel of Strength ... may be expanded and multiplied until the establishment and confirmation of the Holy Kingdom; that the Angel of His Severity ... may continually become more just and more terrible, while the Angel of Mercy ... may always become gentler and more omnipresent, and as His Visible Leader, may have the strength and courage to work tirelessly for the spread of Holy Science and Magnetic Art and Aeonic Magic for the establishment Saints Imperri in the Universe of the World; may not the Providence of Heaven forsake us, nor our weak; so that no one among us should betray, vilify, or violate the cause of the poor and afflicted; so that the Love of Good gathers all the Brothers in one unbreakable bond of the purest Love. Amen.

PREGHIERA QUOTIDIANA DEL CAVALIERE

Signore Santissimo, Padre Omnipotente, Tu che hai permesso sulla Terra l'uso della spada per reprimere la malizia dei malvagi e difendere la giustizia; che per la protezione dei popoli hai voluto istituire l'Ordine della Cavalleria, fa, predisponendo il suo cuore al bene, che Il Tuo servo qui presente non usi mai questa spada o altra per ledere ingiustamente chicchessia, ma se ne serva sempre per difendere la giustizia e il diritto. Amen.

(Translation from the Italian)

KNIGHT'S DAILY PRAYER

Most Holy Lord, Omnipotent Father, You who permitted the use of the sword on Earth to repress the malice of the wicked and defend justice; that for the protection of the peoples you wanted to establish the Order of Chivalry, arrange your heart for good, so that Your servant present here never uses this sword or any other to unjustly harm anyone, but always uses it to defend the justice and law. Amen.

PREGHIER PER L'ASCENSO INDIVIDUALE

Fac, o Anima Intelligens Mundi, ut in studio occultarum legum humani spiritus, degnis admitti fieri possin, fac ut a mi discendant entes spirituales imperfecti, obtenebrantes, et in sensus meos influentes, et ut sergat Sol in oriente psichae meae dormientis, et dux nihi sit mea ipsi voluntas ; fiat lux in conscienta mea.

INVOCAZIONE GNOSTICA O PHTHONO:
ABLANATHANALBA – Padre, vieni a noi!
AGANAKKA – O Forte!
AEIA – Tu Che Sui!
KARNI – Mis forza!
AZREILONEIA – O soccorso Divino!
MOPHAX – Tu che insugfli la vita!
RIOITHEOR – Principe di Luce!
SABAEIAO – Iao Sabaoth!
SEMESE – O Tu, Mediatore!
GNEXIO – Generatore!
KAKO – Storna il male!
SABIRAUGHETA – Sei Valente nel Fuoco!

(Translation from the Italian)

PRAYER BY THE INDIVIDUAL ASCENT

Do, O Intelligent Soul of the World, that in the study of the hidden laws of the human spirit, I may become worthy of admission. Let it be my own will; let there be light in my conscience.

GNOSTIC INVOCATION OR PHTHONO:[140]
ABLANATHANALBA – Father, come to us!
AGANAKKA – O Strong!
AEIA – You Che Sui!
KARNI – My strength!
AZREILONEIA – O Divine help!
MOPHAX – You who breathe life!
RIOITHEOR – Prince of Light!
SABAEIAO – Iao Sabaoth!
SEMESE – O You, Mediator!
GNEXIO – Generator!
KAKO – Avert the evil!
SABIRAUGHETA – You are Valiant in Fire!

---

140 TN: Phthonus – Ancient Greek deity personifying jealousy and envy.

Bibliography

Agrippa, Henry Cornelius (1554) *Fourth Book Of Occult Philosophy*.Marburg. Translated to English by Robert Turner, London: 1655; reprinted by Askin Publishing: 1978; also by Heptangle Books, 1985; and most recently by Ibis Press, 2015, edited with commentary by Stephen Skinner.

Allix (2007) *Manuale dello Studente Magnetizzatore*. Edizioni Rebis (as *Trattato Pratico di Magnetismo Magico*).

Anon (1902) *Clavis Secretorum Celis Et Terrae: Recetas Maravillosas Arte Para Volar Y Para Obtener El Fuego Astral, Etc*. Madrid: Prensa de Madrid; reprinted Miembro de Libris, Asociacion de Libreros de Viejo, 1986. (attributed to Simon Mago or Simon the Magus)

Anon (1969) *Books of Deuteronomy, Joshua, Judges, Ruth, and First Book of Samuel* (Expositions of Holy Scripture). Scranton Company.

Anon (2004) *Holy Bible: King James Version*. Hendrickson Publishing.

Atthel, Dan & Porreca David (intro, trans) (2019) Picatrix: A Medieval Treatise on Angel Magic. PA State University Press.

Barrett, Francis (1801) *The Magus or Celestial Intelligencer*. London: Lackington, Allen, and Co.; reprinted 1875 by Knight and Compton & W. Blackader, most recent edition by Samuel Weiser, Inc. 2000.

Bayard, Jean Pierre (1964) *Le Sacre des Rois*. Editions du vieux colombier Histoire générale.

Caliel (Luigi Petriccione) (1970) *Rituaria di catena terapeutica*. Primo quaderno; Edizione privata.

Caliel (1972) *La magia o pneumatica degli Antichi sia dei Magi del Popolo di Dio che di quelli dei Gentili. Arbatel ; Traduzione e note di Luigi Petriccione*. Corrado Rocco.

Caliel (2011) *Il Sacramentario Segreto*. Edizioni Rebis.

Caliel (2013) *Trattato di Magia Eonica*. Edizioni Rebis.

Caliel (2013) *I Segreti dell'Arte Reale*. Edizioni Rebis.

Caliel (2019) *La Magia degli Dei*. Edizioni Rebis.

Conybeare, Frederick (trans) (1898) *Testament of Solomon The King*. London: 1898, 'Jewish Quarterly Review', volume II.

Crowley, Aleister (1904) *Book of the Goetia of Solomon the King*. Foyers, Inverness: Society for the Propagation of Religious Truth.

Davies, Owen (2009) *Grimoires: A History of Magic Books*. Oxford: Oxford University Press.

Dehn, Georg (ed) & Guth, Steven (trans) (2006/2015) *The Book of Abramelin.* Ibis Press.

Eliade, Mircea (1979/81) *History of Religious Ideas.* Chicago: University of Chicago Press.

Encausse, Gerard (Papus) (ND) *Traite Elementaire de Science Occulte.* Paris: Edition Dangles.

Encausse, Gerard (2018) *Elementary Treatise of Occult Science.* Minnesota: Llewelyn Publishing.

Evola, Julius & the Ur Group, Moynihan, Michael (ed) (1971, 2001) *Introduction to Magic, Volume I: Rituals and Practical Techniques for the Magus.* Inner Traditions.

Evola, Julius & the Ur Group, Godwin, Josceyln (trans) (1971, 2019) *Introduction to Magic, Volume II: The Path of Initiatic Wisdom.* Inner Traditions.

Evola, Julius & the Ur Group, Godwin, Josceyln (trans) (1971, 2021) *Introduction to Magic, Volume III: Realizations of the Absolute Individual.* Inner Traditions.

Gardner, Gerald (2015) *Ye Bok of ye Art Magical.* Blurb Inc.

Group of Ur (2021) *La Dimensione Magica del Gruppo di Ur.* Edizioni Rebis.

Hockley, Frederick (2011) *Book of the Offices of Spirits: The Occult Virtue of Plants and Some Rare Magical Charms and Spells.* Teitan Press.

Hubert, Henri & Mauss, Marcel (1999) *Essay on Time: A Brief Study of the Representation of Time in Religion and Magic.* Durkheim Press Ltd.

Johnson, Brian (trans) (2019) *Testament of Solomon, Recension C.* Keighley: Hadean Press.

Levi, Eliphas (1975/2000) *Great Secret or Occultism Unveiled.* York Beach, ME.

Levi, Eliphas (1973/1977) *Book of Splendours: The Inner Mysteries Of Qabalism.* Aquarian Press/Samuel Weiser Inc., 1973/1977.

Levi, Eliphas (1959) *Key of the Mysteries.* London: Rider Co.

Levi, Eliphas (1898) *Le Grand Arcane ou l'Occultisme Devoile.*

Levi, Eliphas (1896) *Transcendental Magic: It's Doctrine And Ritual.* London: George Redway, reprinted Chicago, IL: De Laurence Co. 1910.

Levi, Eliphas (1896) *Magical Ritual of the Sanctum Regnum.* London: George Redway.

Maclaren, Alexander (ed) (1969) Peterson, Joseph (trans) (2009) *Arbatel: Concerning The Magic Of The Ancients.* Ibis Press.

Mathers, S.L.MacGregor (trans) (1889) *Key Of Solomon The King.* London: George Redway; reprinted by Kegan Paul, Trench, Trubner and Co., 1909; also by Chicago: De Laurence Publishing, 1914.

Mathers, S.L.MacGregor (trans) (1898) *Book Of The Sacred Magic Of Abra-Melin The Mage.* London: John Watkins, 1898; reprinted 1939/1948 by De Laurence Publishing, Chicago, IL; plus various other editions.

Peterson, Joseph (ed, trans) (2017) *La Veritable Magie Noire: True Black Magic*. Kasson, MN: Twilit Grotto Press.

Peterson, Joseph (ed, trans) (2016) *The Sworn Book of Honorius*. Lake Worth, FL: Ibis Press.

Peterson, Joseph (ed) (2007) *Grimorium Verum*. CreateSpace Publishing, 2007.

Peterson, Joseph (ed) (2001) *Lesser Key Of Solomon: Lemegeton Clavicula Salomonis: Detailing The Ceremonial Art Of Commanding Spirits Both Good And Evil*. York Beach, ME: Weiser Books.

Pierini, Pier Luca (ed) (2017) *Il Tesoro Magico Del Re Salomone*. Edizioni Rebis.

Pierini, Pier Luca (ed) (2013) *Il Vero Libro Delle Ombre: Liber Umbrarum Vel Liber Spirituuam; Verum Divinum Grimoirium*. Edizioni Rebis.

Pierini, Pier Luca (ed) (2003) *Lo Scrigno Dei Segreti Magici Del Salomone*. Edizioni Rebis.

Pierini, Pier Luca (ed) (2000-2014) *Magia Segreta* (8 volumes). Edizioni Rebis.

Pierini, Pier Luca (ed) (1982) *Arbatel, o la Magia degli Antichi*. Edizioni Rebis.

Piobb, Pierre Vincenti (1937/1977) *Formulaire de Haute Magie*. Paris: Editions Dangles.

Rankine, David (ed) (2013) *The Complete Grimoire of Pope Honorius*. Avalonia.

Shah, Idries (1957) *Secret Lore of Magic*. Frederick Muller Ltd.

Skinner, Stephen & Rankine, David (eds) (2008) *The Veritable Key of Solomon*. Singapore: Golden Hoard Press.

Skinner, Stephen & Rankine, David (eds) (2007) *The Goetia of Dr. Rudd*. Singapore: Golden Hoard Press.

Sullivan, Matthew (trans) (1999) *Great Grimoire Of Pope Honourius*. Trident Books.

Turner, Robert (trans) (2003) *Heptameron Or Magical Elements of Peter de Abano & Arbatel Or the Magick of the Ancients*. Seattle, WA: Ouroboros Press.

Van Der Leeuw (1933) *Phenomenology Der Religion*. J. C. B. Mohr (Paul Siebeck), Tubingen.

Waite, Arthur Edward (1898) *The Book Of Black Magic And Pacts*. London.

Waite, Arthur Edward (1911) *Book of Ceremonial Magic*. London: Rider Publishing.

Weyer, Johann & Zasadzinska (trans) (2015-16) *The False Hierarchy of Demons*. Abracax House.

Weyer, Johann & Mora, George (ed) & Kohl, Benjamin (ed) (1991) *Witches, Devils & Doctors in the Renaissance*. Medieval & Renaissance Texts & Studies. The first English translation of 'De Praestigiis Daemonum'.

www.ingramcontent.com/pod-product-compliance
Lightning Source LLC
Chambersburg PA
CBHW060923170426
43192CB00021B/2855